COFFEE-TIME QUILTS

Super Projects, Sweet Recipes

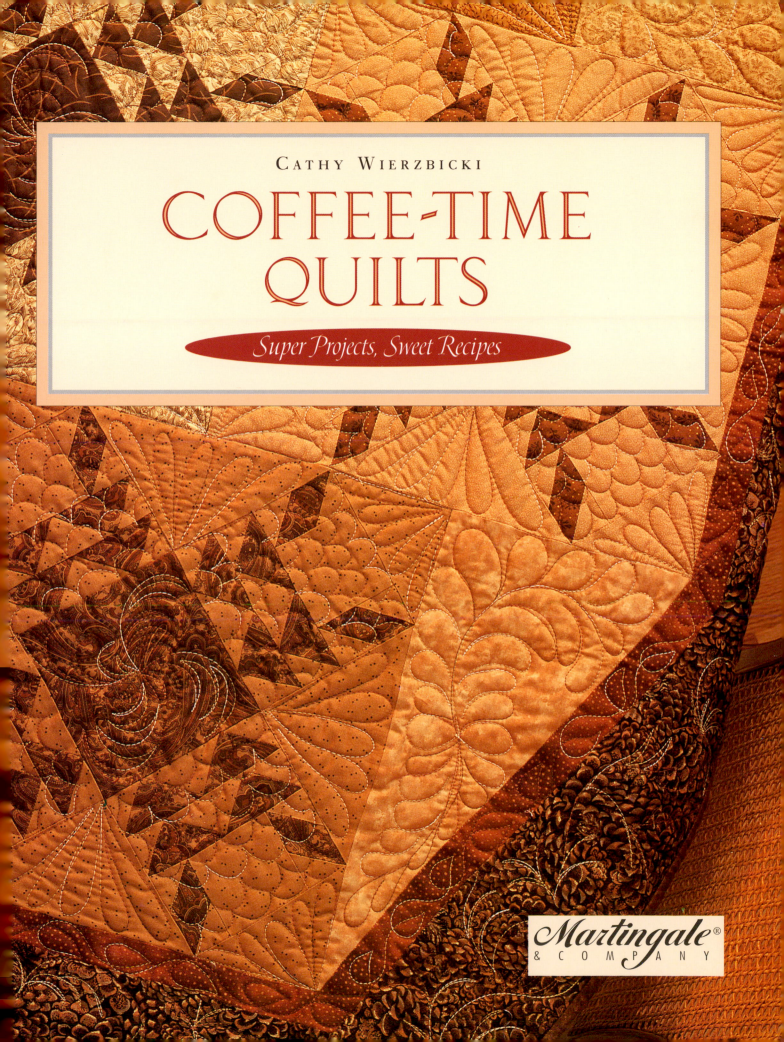

CATHY WIERZBICKI

COFFEE-TIME QUILTS

Super Projects, Sweet Recipes

Martingale® & COMPANY

Coffee-Time Quilts: Super Projects, Sweet Recipes
© 2004 Cathy Wierzbicki

That Patchwork Place® is an imprint of Martingale & Company®.

Martingale & Company
20205 144th Avenue NE
Woodinville, WA 98072-8478
www.martingale-pub.com

Printed in China
09 08 07 06 05 04   8 7 6 5 4 3 2 1

Library of Congress Cataloging-in-Publication Data

Wierzbicki, Cathy.
    Coffee-time quilts: super projects, sweet recipes / Cathy
Wierzbicki.
        p. cm.
    ISBN 1-56477-525-9
    1. Patchwork—Patterns. 2. Quilting—Patterns. 3. Coffee in art.
4. Desserts. I. Title.
    TT835 .W532 2004
    746.46'041—dc22

                                2003021767

Mission Statement
Dedicated to providing quality products
and service to inspire creativity.

Credits

President ♦ *Nancy J. Martin*
CEO ♦ *Daniel J. Martin*
Publisher ♦ *Jane Hamada*
Editorial Director ♦ *Mary V. Green*
Managing Editor ♦ *Tina Cook*
Technical Editor ♦ *Laurie Baker*
Copy Editor ♦ *Mary R. Martin*
Design Director ♦ *Stan Green*
Illustrator ♦ *Brian Metz*
Cover and Text Designer ♦ *Trina Stahl*
Photographer ♦ *Brent Kane*

Dedication

I am honored to dedicate this book to my mother and friend, Shirley Sullivan. It is because of her encouragement that I began the journey down the path of quiltmaking. Even though we are separated by distance, she will always be close to my heart.

Acknowledgments

Very special thanks to:

April West of Ames, Iowa, who machine quilted all of the designs in this book except "Freeze-Dried Crystals" and "Cups and Saucers." Her artistic talent with needle and thread enhances every quilt she touches.

Pam Clarke of Spokane, Washington, whose creative machine quilting on "Freeze-Dried Crystals" makes this quilt sparkle. Her work is beautiful.

Hobbs Bonded Fibers, Bernina of America, and YLI Corporation for their fine products.

The talented and dedicated Martingale & Company staff. They are leaders in quilting excellence.

I would also like to thank:

A special group of quilting friends in Ankeny, Iowa: Tamara Watts, Rita Bigelow, Shelley Mitchell, Ilene Bartos, and Janeen Pearson, who have supported and encouraged me in all of my quilting endeavors for years.

Margaret Graham and Tammy Rondorf for their friendship and for assisting with the photo props.

Henrietta Wierzbicki, the greatest mother-in-law a girl could ask for. She fills our hearts with her love and our bellies with her wonderful recipes. Her delicious coffee cake recipe is featured on page 85.

My daughter, Stacey, and son, Tom, who bring balance to my life and remind me there is a world outside of quilting.

My husband, Tom, for more than 30 years of love, encouragement, and comic relief. Wherever the road leads us, I feel fortunate beyond measure to be making my life's journey with him.

CONTENTS

Introduction ♦ 9
Quiltmaking Ingredients ♦ 11
Quiltmaking Recipes ♦ 14
Finishing Touches ♦ 20

ROBUST ROASTS
Projects in warm, toasty hues

Cappuccino Crossroads ♦ 26
Caramel Latte ♦ 30
Freeze-Dried Crystals ♦ 36
Double-Shot Mocha Cheesecake ♦ 42
Mocha Chocolate-Cherry Chewies ♦ 43

JAVA JOLT
Quilts with a kick of color and vitality

Espresso to Go ♦ 46
Hearty Blend ♦ 50
Hearty Blend Lite ♦ 54
One Lump or Two? ♦ 58
Caramel Latte Cake ♦ 63
Cups and Saucers Table Runner ♦ 64
Cups and Saucers Place Mats ♦ 68

DECAFFEINATED DELIGHTS
Soothing and relaxing designs

Totally Decaffeinated ♦ 74
Percolating Pinwheels ♦ 80
Mom's Cinnamon-Pecan Coffee Cake ♦ 85
Service for Four ♦ 86
Blueberry Coffee Cake ♦ 93

About the Author ♦ 95

INTRODUCTION

RECENTLY, MY HUSBAND and I relocated to the Pacific Northwest from the plains of Iowa. Despite the obvious differences in weather, lifestyle, and geography, it became apparent that there was at least one profound similarity—both areas have rich quilting traditions. I immediately knew I would feel right at home as long as there were fabric stores and quilters nearby.

Many of my previous quilts were inspired by life in the Midwest, and I began to wonder how my inspirations would change in a new home surrounded by the majesty and beauty of snow-capped mountains and vast ocean waters teeming with marine life. But the one image that kept percolating in my mind was of coffee. In fact, coffee has a strong presence in this part of the country. With a coffee shop on seemingly every street corner, this area is undoubtedly home to the world's highest number of coffee establishments per capita!

This book combines several of my favorite things: warm and cozy quilts, robust coffee, and delicious recipes. If a quilt book built around the theme of coffee conjures images of black, brown, or otherwise dark quilts, think again. This book is brimming with bright and spirited designs and cooking recipes, full of body and warmth, with just the right blend for quilters of all skill levels. I've indicated the required skill level—easy, moderate, or more challenging—for each quilt.

☕ = Easy   ☕ ☕ = Moderate   ☕ ☕ ☕ = More Challenging

Although this book is built around a hot, timely theme, the primary emphasis is a variety of imaginative quilts that include classic blocks as well as a few original ones. While some of the quilts evoke the feeling of a robust roast, others offer an extra kick of color, and still others provide a calming, soothing, and totally decaffeinated effect. The projects range from small wall hangings and table toppers to queen-size bed quilts. And be sure to set aside some time to try a few of the tasty recipes that will leave your mouth watering for more.

As you pore over these designs, I am confident you, too, will warm up to the notion of a coffee-theme quilt and brew one up for yourself. It has "bean" a pleasure! From the bottom of my grateful heart, thank you for making this book part of your quilting library.

May you always take time to quilt,

Cathy

QUILTMAKING INGREDIENTS

YESTERDAY'S QUILTERS produced countless beautiful works of art using minimal sewing aids, often making a quilt entirely by hand. Some quilters today continue to piece and quilt by hand. However, quiltmaking has evolved into an enormous, specialized industry that offers quilters a wide array of tools and gadgets to choose from. But you need only a few high-quality, carefully selected tools to produce a modern-day beauty.

SEWING MACHINE

ONCE you have decided that a sewing machine is essential to your quiltmaking, *don't skimp on the sewing machine.* I'm not suggesting you mortgage the farm to buy a sewing machine, but I believe you should buy the best machine your budget will afford. Consider it an investment. After all, you will need to purchase very few sewing machines throughout an entire lifetime if you choose wisely. A good day in the sewing room will quickly turn sour with a temperamental sewing machine. Select a high-quality machine that offers features geared toward quiltmaking. And, by all means, take the classes offered by the retail sewing-machine merchants so that you can learn how to use your machine *before* you go to a retreat or workshop!

FABRIC

SOME quilters have trouble with fabric selection, but it is really quite easy if you follow a few simple "rules":

♦ Buy only high-quality 100% cotton fabrics.
♦ If you like it, buy it.
♦ If you *really* like it, buy more of it.

As the sign in my favorite quilt store says, "Buy it today . . . it might not be here tomorrow."

I have been known to let my fabric "age" on the shelf for a while, but it is a good idea to use the fabric while the colors are still in style and while you are still attracted to the fabric. Over time, our tastes change and fabric we once just had to have no longer holds the same appeal.

When choosing fabrics, consider including a variety of scales, prints, and colors in the same quilt. A diversity of shades, values, and textures adds interest. Some quilters find it helpful to take their cues from the main print, which could be a floral, paisley, or other patterned fabric. Often referred to as the "focus" fabric, this is the dominant print from which all other companion fabrics are selected. Simply choose fabrics that match colors in the focus fabric and you will almost always be assured of having good companions. If you buy fabrics and colors that you like, chances are you'll be pleased with the finished product.

I confess I do not always prewash my fabrics, especially when working with small cuts of fabric. I know, however, that there is a certain element of risk associated with not prewashing. Most days I feel lucky, but someday I'll suffer the consequences of a red that runs or a blue that goes gray. When that happens, I'll make another quilt. To minimize the risks of fabric bleeding, my best advice is to prewash dark and light fabrics in separate loads, rinsing until the water runs clear. To help set the colors, a little splash of vinegar in the final rinse doesn't hurt.

THREAD

PURCHASE high-quality, cotton or cotton-covered polyester thread for patchwork piecing. Neutral beige and medium gray are versatile and blend with most fabric combinations. With so many threads available today, you might want to experiment with a variety of them to evaluate how they perform with your machine and how they look in your quilt. If the bobbin case of your machine seems to become full of lint, it could be that you are using low-quality thread or inferior-quality fabric.

PINS AND NEEDLES

PINS are another one of those notions about which quilters have strong feelings. You can't go wrong if you select rustproof pins that are easy to handle. For me, that means pins that have a small beadlike head and a sharp point that is free of burrs. Beaded heads are easy to grip and easy to find if they're dropped on the floor.

When selecting needles for your sewing machine, use those recommended by your machine's manufacturer. My best advice is to use a sharp needle. If your needle starts to sound "clunky" when sewing, it is probably past the time for a new needle.

For hand-sewing needles, choose a high-quality needle that will glide through fabric and enhance your sewing experience. For hand quilting, use a size 8 to 12 Between. The higher the needle size, the smaller the needle. Novice quilters usually begin with size 8 or 10, moving up to a smaller needle as they become more experienced. For hand appliqué, I prefer to use very thin, high-quality English Sharps in a size 10 or 12. If your needle seems to be dragging through the fabric, pull the needle through a scrap of wool quilt batting. The lanolin in the wool lubricates the needle, which is why hand quilting on a wool batting is such a pleasure.

SCISSORS

I NEVER met a pair of scissors I didn't like, but as with your other tools, the key is to purchase scissors of high quality. Many new styles of scissors are available. Choose the kind that appeals to you, use them only on fabric, and keep them sharp. Keep another pair strictly for use on paper. Also, consider purchasing a pair of small "snips" for trimming threads.

ROTARY CUTTING TOOLS

IF there is a better tool for quiltmaking than a sharp rotary cutter, I can't imagine what it would be! They are available in a variety of styles and sizes; choosing one is a matter of personal preference. Safety is of paramount importance when working with rotary cutting tools. If you have grown attached to your toes, do not use a rotary cutter while you are barefoot. If you ever drop a rotary cutter with an open blade you will quickly learn how much damage can be done when a razor-sharp edge falls onto an unsuspecting pinkie.

Select a clear, acrylic ruler with features that you like. My best advice is to purchase one that is about 24" long and 6" wide with ⅛" markings and at least a 45°-angle line drawn on it. This size works well in most cases. As your quilting wish list grows, you might want to add a smaller ruler, as well as an acrylic square. Many of the other specialized acrylic tools on the market are also very useful, and they help to simplify some cutting tasks, but they are not essential for the quilts in this book.

Self-healing mats are essential when using rotary cutters. While they are self-healing, they are not cut-proof. Over time, your mat will begin to show signs of wear and will need to be replaced. Extend the life of your mat by maintaining a sharp cutter. Several mat sizes are available. For most situations, a mat that is about 24" x 16" is a good all-purpose choice.

COFFEE FACTS

♦ Coffee is the second-most-traded commodity in the world economy, surpassed only by oil.

♦ Of the American population over 18 years of age, 107 million drink coffee every day, and 57 million drink coffee occasionally.

♦ One coffee tree yields slightly less than one pound of coffee per year.

♦ Coffee drinkers consume an average of 3.3 cups of coffee per day.

♦ Men drink as much coffee as women.

QUILTMAKING RECIPES

THIS SECTION COVERS those morsels of basic information you need in order to sew a successful project. Techniques used for piecing and finishing the quilts throughout the book can be found here, but feel free to use methods from your own quilting recipe box as well.

ACCURATE SEAM ALLOWANCES

SEVERAL variables can affect patchwork outcome, including the accuracy of cutting and pressing patchwork pieces. However, the greatest secret to patchwork success is mastering the ¼" seam allowance. Here is a little exercise to test the accuracy of your seam allowance.

1. Cut three 1½" x 6" strips of any scrap fabric.

2. Using a ¼" seam allowance, sew the strips together along the long edges.

3. Measure the finished width of the center strip. If it is precisely 1", you passed the test. If the finished width of the center strip yields any measurement other than 1", you need to adjust your technique and retest. Any distortion in seam allowance is magnified several times across a particular block, and magnified many more times across an entire quilt top. If your blocks do not fit together properly, or if recommended border sizes do not fit your quilt top,

chances are pretty good that your seam allowance is at fault.

HALF-SQUARE AND QUARTER-SQUARE TRIANGLES

AMONG the most basic shapes in quiltmaking are half-square and quarter-square triangles. Once you commit the following easy math formulas to memory, you will always know how to calculate the correct size square to cut from your fabric whenever you want half-square and quarter-square triangles.

Half-square triangles are made by cutting a square in half once diagonally. Each square yields two triangles. The *short* edges of each triangle are on the straight of grain. To calculate the size square to cut, first determine the finished size of the triangle's short side, then add ⅞" for seam allowances. Cut a square the determined size, and then cut it in half diagonally from corner to corner. For example, if the finished size of a unit is 2", cut a square 2⅞" and then cut it in half diagonally.

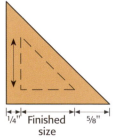

¼" Finished size   ⅝"

¼" + ⅝" = ⅞"

Quarter-square triangles are made by cutting a square in half twice diagonally. Each square yields four triangles. The *long* edge of each triangle is on the straight of grain. To figure out what size the initial square should be, determine the finished measurement of the triangle's long side; then add 1¼" for seam allowances. Cut a square of the determined size. Next cut it in half diagonally from corner to corner and then in half again on the opposite diagonal. For example, if the finished size of a unit is 2", cut a square 3¼" and then cut it in half twice diagonally.

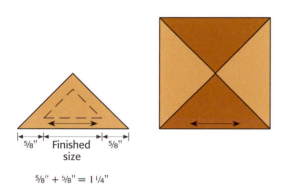

5/8" + 5/8" = 1 1/4"

FABRIC GRAIN LINE

THE grain of fabric refers to the direction of the yarns used to weave the fabric. The yarns in the crosswise grain run from selvage to selvage. Pieces cut on the crosswise grain have a little bit of stretch, or "give," to them. Lengthwise yarns have no stretch and produce pieces that are very stable. Have you ever seen a quilt with wavy or rippled edges? Chances are the borders of the quilt were cut across the grain of the fabric and have stretched along the edges, resulting in a quilt that "waves" at you. While this makes for a very "friendly" quilt, it isn't ideal.

While cutting the pieces along the lengthwise grain creates the most stable quilt, it usually requires more yardage and results in more leftovers. For the purposes of this book, I have elected to cut all but the outer border pieces along the crosswise grain in most instances. Therefore, when sewing strips that have been cut across the grain, be aware that they can become distorted. Use extra care to avoid stretching the strips so that you do not end up with a "friendly" quilt.

APPLIQUÉ TECHNIQUES

THIS book presents two small projects that use appliqué. There are many techniques for doing appliqué; I have included four in this section. The fusible-web method is quick and easy, using an iron and machine stitching, while the other three methods use more traditional hand-stitching techniques. If you would like to explore other appliqué techniques, Martingale & Company has published many excellent books devoted entirely to appliqué, and I encourage you to ask for them at your local quilt shop or bookstore.

Fusible-Web Appliqué

In this method, fusible webbing is used to adhere the shape to the background. Decorative machine stitching is then applied to the motif edges.

Fusible web has smooth paper on one side that is protecting an iron-on adhesive, and an exposed iron-on adhesive on the other. It comes in several weights, but for the motifs in this book, I recommend a lightweight fusible web that can easily be stitched through. General instructions for adhering the shape to the fabric are included here, but always follow the manufacturer's guidelines for the fusible product you are using.

It is important to note that this method produces an image that is the reverse of the pattern given in the book. In other words, if you are tracing a left-facing coffee mug pattern from this book, the mug will face right when completed. The patterns are presented so that they will be facing the correct direction when applied using this method. If you want to reverse the direction of any template pattern, simply trace it from the back side of the pattern rather than the front side. It is not necessary to reverse the pattern when working with symmetrical shapes, such as the heart template for "Hearty Blend Lite."

1. Place the appliqué pattern on a flat surface. Position the fusible webbing on top of the pattern, paper side up. Trace the pattern onto the paper side of the webbing. Remember, the pattern has already been reversed so that it will be facing the correct direction when it is applied to the background.

2. Roughly cut around the appliqué shape, cutting about ⅛" from the drawn line. Place the fusible web side of the shape on the wrong side of the appropriate fabric and press it in place, following the manufacturer's instructions. Allow it to cool.

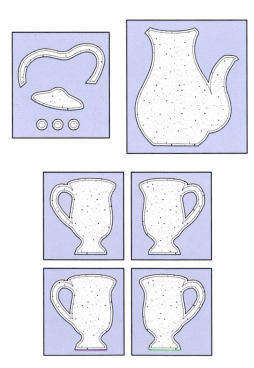

3. Cut out the shape on the drawn line and remove the paper backing.

4. With the adhesive side down, position the appliqué shape on the right side of the background fabric and press.

5. Using a small zigzag or buttonhole stitch, machine stitch around each appliqué shape.

Freezer-Paper Appliqué

I am particularly fond of this appliqué technique. Because the freezer paper is basted to the appliqué shape, the paper cannot come loose. This makes the project pieces very stable and portable for traveling.

Freezer paper is a heavy-duty white paper that is plastic-coated on one side. It is sold on a roll in grocery stores and some quilt shops. In grocery stores, look for it in the aisle where plastic wraps and garbage bags are found.

Like fusible-web appliqué, this method produces a finished appliqué that is the reverse of the pattern.

1. Place the appliqué pattern on a flat surface. Position a piece of freezer paper on top of the pattern, shiny side down, and trace the pattern onto it.

2. Cut out the freezer-paper shape on the drawn line.

3. Press the freezer-paper shape, shiny side down, onto the wrong side of the appropriate fabric.

4. Trim around the fabric shape, adding ⅛" to ¼" seam allowance.

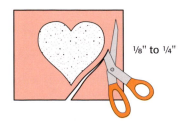

⅛" to ¼"

5. Using a contrasting thread and a running stitch, baste around the entire shape, turning under and catching the seam allowance as you go.

Fold.

6. Position the shape on the background.

7. Using a needle threaded with a color that closely matches the appliqué piece, sew the shape into place with small stitches. Start by bringing the needle up through the background fabric and through the edge of the basted appliqué fabric. Insert the needle back down through the background fabric and repeat the same stitch about ⅛" away from the first stitch. Continue stitching in this manner all around the appliqué shape and extending a few stitches past the spot where you began. Knot the thread on the wrong side of the background fabric.

Appliqué Stitch

8. Clip the contrasting basting thread and remove it from the appliqué piece.

9. Working from the wrong side of the background fabric, carefully make a small slit behind the appliqué piece and remove the freezer paper. Use caution to avoid cutting through the appliqué piece.

Needle-Turn Appliqué—Paper on Top

The advantage of this technique is that you do not have to do any basting. The disadvantage is that even though you are using a freezer-paper shape, it can come loose from the fabric if it is not handled gently. This technique produces an appliqué that *is not the reverse of the pattern.*

1. Trace the appliqué pattern onto a sheet of plain paper so it is facing the direction it needs to be when it is stitched to the background. Place the traced appliqué pattern on a flat surface. Position a piece of freezer paper on top of the pattern, shiny side down, and trace the pattern onto it.

2. Cut out the freezer-paper shape on the drawn line.

3. Press the shiny side of the freezer-paper shape onto the right side of the appropriate fabric.

4. Trim around the freezer-paper template, adding ⅛" to ¼" for seam allowance.

⅛" to ¼"

5. Position the appliqué piece on the background fabric, paper side up, and pin it in place.

6. Using the edge of the freezer-paper shape as a guide, use the point of your needle to turn under the seam allowance of the fabric. Refer to step 7 of "Freezer-Paper Appliqué" at left to stitch the appliqué shape into place.

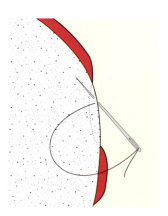

7. Remove the freezer paper.

Needle-Turn Appliqué—No Paper on Top

The advantage of this technique is that the pattern lines are traced directly onto the appliqué fabric, around a freezer-paper template. The disadvantage is that you must carefully turn under the seam allowance to conceal the drawn lines. This method also produces an appliqué that *is not the reverse of the pattern*.

1. Trace the appliqué pattern onto a sheet of plain paper so it is facing the direction it needs to be when it is stitched to the background. Place the traced appliqué pattern on a flat surface. Position a piece of freezer paper on top of the pattern, shiny side down, and trace the pattern onto it.

2. Cut out the freezer-paper template on the drawn line.

3. Place the template on the right side of the appropriate fabric and trace around it, using a very sharp pencil or water-soluble pen. Remove the template.

4. Cut around the drawn lines, adding ⅛" to ¼" seam allowance.

⅛" to ¼"

5. Pin the appliqué shape in place.

6. Using the point of your needle, turn under the seam allowance of the fabric, taking care to conceal the drawn line. Refer to step 7 of

"Freezer-Paper Appliqué" on page 16 to stitch the appliqué shape into place.

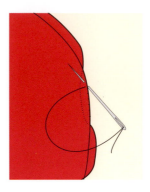

QUILT ASSEMBLY

To assemble a quilt, begin by sewing the blocks into rows, and then sew the rows together. As you construct the rows, press the seams of each row in opposite directions.

The simplest block arrangement is the straight set, in which blocks are sewn into straight rows.

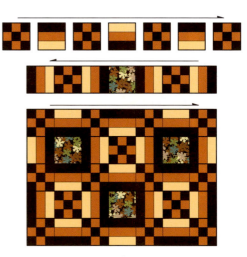

Straight Set

For on-point settings, in which blocks are positioned diagonally, sew the side triangles to the ends of the rows, join the rows, and then attach the corner triangles.

Diagonal Set

When working with large quilts, I often find it helpful to construct the quilt in quarter sections and then sew the quarter sections together.

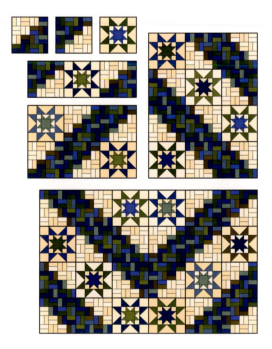

BORDERS

AFTER the center blocks are assembled, it is time to add the borders. The project instructions indicate the exact size to cut the border strips. The border measurements are based on the length that the top, bottom, and side edges of the quilt top should be if a ¼" seam allowance was maintained throughout construction of the quilt top. *Before you cut,* it is always a good practice to measure the quilt top through the center to determine its *actual* dimensions and then adjust the border measurements as necessary.

The outer borders for all of the quilts are cut on the lengthwise grain to prevent wavy edges. Some inner borders are cut on the crosswise grain and will need to be pieced together to achieve the required length. To reduce bulk in the seams, miter the strips together. Trim the seam allowances to ¼".

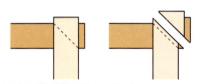

FINISHING TOUCHES

Y OU'RE ALMOST DONE. Once you have the backing prepared and the batting select‑ed, making the quilt sandwich is next. Then it's on to quilting, binding, and making a label.

PREPARING THE BACKING

THE back of your quilt provides a wonderful opportunity to exercise a little extra creativi‑ty in your quiltmaking. Rather than use a solid piece of fabric on the back, consider using a variety of fabrics to add interest and help camouflage quilting that might be less than perfect. The back is also a good place to put any extra blocks or pieced elements that were not used on the front. In addition to providing a surprise on the back, there is a practical reason to use elements from the front as well. In the event of damage to the front, you can easily extract a piece of the exact fabric from the back and transplant it to the front to repair the quilt.

When preparing the backing, always make it several inches larger than the quilt top (I prefer about 4" larger on all sides). The oversized backing provides the extra fabric necessary when using a hoop or frame for quilting.

CHOOSING BATTING

CHOOSING a batting to use in your quilt can depend on several variables, including the size of the quilt, its intended use, the amount of quilting to be done, the color of fabrics used, whether it will be quilted by hand or machine, the content of the batting, and many other considerations. There are few absolutes regarding batting. Thicker batting is sometimes actually easier to quilt through than thin, dense batting. One of the easiest battings to hand quilt through is washable wool, despite its loft. The natural lanolin in the batting lubricates the needle, allowing it to glide through the fabrics. Battings of

100% cotton are thinner, but denser, and much more difficult for me to needle by hand, yet they offer advantages not found in polyester batting. Some polyester or polyester-cotton blend battings are acceptable. My best advice is to try several high-quality battings and evaluate them for yourself, remembering to follow the manufacturer's directions. Stick with the batting that is most pleasing to you.

LAYERING AND BASTING

PLACE the backing wrong side up on a clean, flat surface and secure it with masking tape or binder clips. Keep the backing taut, but be careful not to stretch it out of shape or the finished project may have puckers. Position the batting over the backing and smooth it in place. Center the quilt top over the batting, right side up. Baste the layers together. Thread basting works best for hand quilting. For machine quilting, use rustproof safety pins.

QUILTING

ONE of the ways quiltmaking has evolved is with the wide acceptance of machine quilting. Finishing a quilt requires several decisions, including whether to quilt by hand or machine and what quilting motifs to use. This part of the quiltmaking process can be an entire book unto itself. There are countless methods, marking tools, stencils, and designs available. My best advice is to investigate different resources and experiment with the variety of aids available. Alternatively, you can rely on the expertise of talented machine quilting professionals to make those decisions for you.

PAINLESS MITERED BINDING

EVEN though putting on the binding signals the completion of a quilt, most quilters do not enjoy this quiltmaking task. Perhaps you have applied binding using your preferred method only to end up with an outcome that is less than satisfactory. Or perhaps you don't care to deal with how to make the last miter joint where the two open ends of the binding come together. The mitered binding method presented here eliminates those issues and makes binding totally painless. The result is mitered corners that are already machine-sewn on both the front and back so that you do not have to stitch them by hand when you turn the corner while sewing down the binding. In fact, the corners almost magically turn by themselves, giving you perfect mitered corners every time.

Another benefit of this method is that it works with binding of any width. You do not have to make any adjustments when sewing—you simply cut the binding strips wider. If you try this method just once, I believe it will become your new best friend in quiltmaking.

1. Place a chalk mark ¼" from each corner of the quilt top and measure the quilt top between the marks.

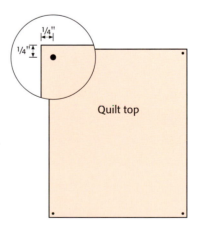

2. Cut strips from the binding fabric. This technique will work for binding of any width, provided all the strips are the same width. In general, for very thin binding, cut strips 2⅛" wide across the width of the fabric. For wider binding, cut strips approximately 2½" to 2¾" wide across the width of the fabric.

3. For each edge of the quilt, you will need one strip that is approximately 6" longer than the edge to be bound. Join strips, if necessary, to make a long enough strip.

4. Press the strips in half lengthwise, wrong sides together.

5. With the raw edges even, sew a folded strip to one edge of the quilt top, leaving approximately 3" of binding extending beyond each end. Begin sewing at the first chalk mark; stop sewing at the second chalk mark. Backstitch to secure the ends. We will refer to this point later as the "tacked stitch."

6. Repeat step 5 for each side.

7. Here is where the magic happens. Prepare a "miter marking guide." To prepare the guide, draw a diagonal line from corner to corner on a 3" square self-stick note. Using a ruler, at one corner where the diagonal line intersects, make seven to eight pencil marks along the two adjacent edges as shown, spacing the marks approximately ⅛" apart.

8. Place the raw edge of one of the binding strips on a flat surface in front of you. Bring the folded edge of the binding to the stitching line and make a crease mark. Open up the binding and lay it flat again.

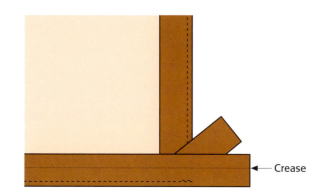

9. Place the "miter marking guide" on the binding strip, aligning the diagonal line of the paper with the crease mark on the binding. Position the marking tool so that one of the ⅛" markings meets the folded edge of the binding and so that another of the ⅛" markings meets the tacked stitch of the binding. *There should be an equal number of marks from the tip of the sticky note to the folded edge of the binding and from the tip of the sticky note to the tacked stitch of the binding.*

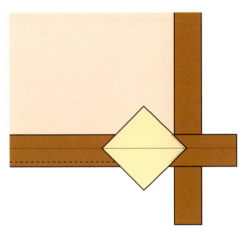

10. Using a pencil or chalk marker, trace around the marked corner of the marking guide, drawing a line from the folded edge of the binding to the tacked stitch. Remove the marking guide. With the right side of the quilt facing up, fold the quilt diagonally from the corner so that the marked binding strip and the adjacent binding strip are aligned along the folded edges. Pin the binding strips together.

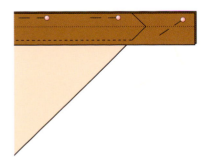

11. Sew along the marked line, starting at the folded edge of the binding and stitching up to the tip. Take one stitch across the point of the tip and continue sewing down the marked line to the tacked stitch. Trim ¼" from the stitching line and turn the corner to the right side.

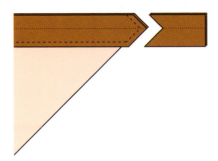

12. Repeat for the remaining corners.

LABELING

I RECOMMEND documenting your quilts by using two methods. First, always sign and date your quilt using a permanent ink marker suitable for fabric. I do this directly on the back (or sometimes, the front) of the quilt. In addition, I add a label and usually apply it directly over the penned signature. In the event a label comes loose or is removed, the penned signature will remain permanently. Labels are the best way to document your quilt and pass along important or interesting information for future generations. Every quilt has a story to tell, yet many of them are being denied a voice because they have no label. Labels do not have to be fancy; a plain piece of muslin and permanent fabric pens will get the job done. (Of course, you are encouraged to be a little more creative than that.) Consider including the following information on your label: quiltmaker's full name; the date the quilt was made; city where it was made; who it was given to or made for, if applicable; the occasion for making it, such as a birth, wedding, or anniversary; and any other information about the quilt that future generations will find interesting. Attach the label to the back of the quilt just as you would an appliqué piece.

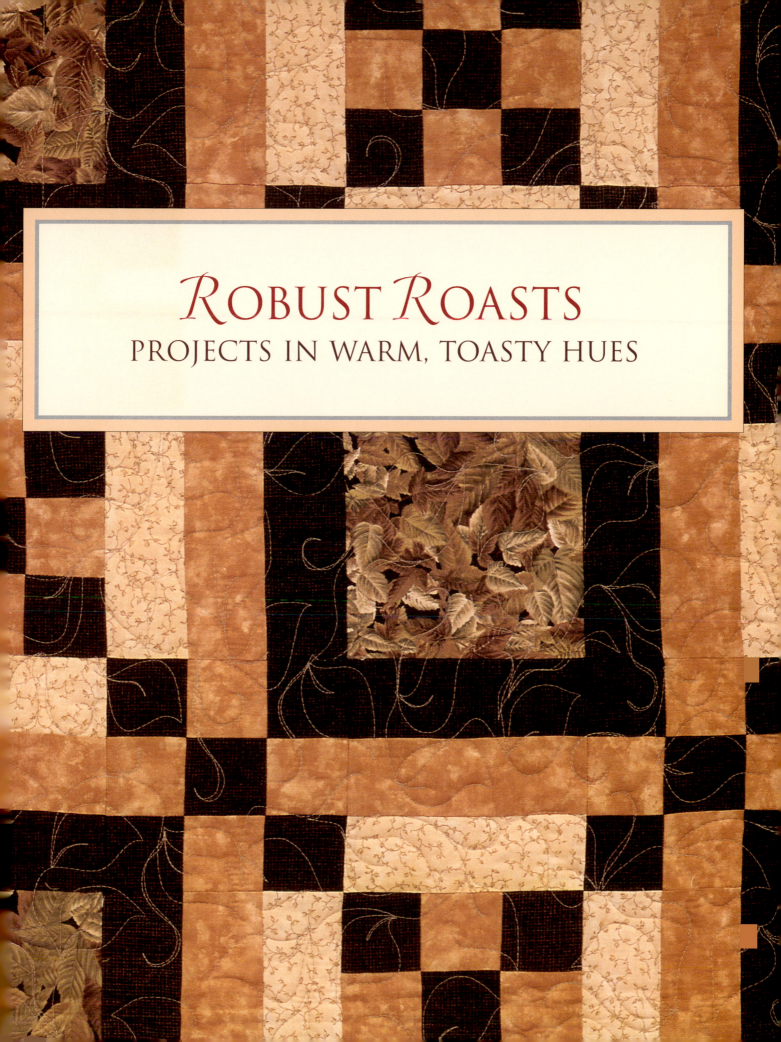

Robust Roasts

PROJECTS IN WARM, TOASTY HUES

CAPPUCCINO CROSSROADS

CLASSIC NINE PATCH blocks are paired with simple Rail Fence blocks and large squares of the focus fabric in this very easy quilt that only looks difficult. Everything about this quilt is easy, from selecting the fabric to constructing the blocks.

SKILL LEVEL:

Plain Square Block   Rail Fence Block   Nine Patch Block

MAIN INGREDIENTS

Yardage is based on 42"-wide fabric unless otherwise noted. Select the main fabric first, and then select three companion fabrics consisting of a light, a medium, and a dark.

- 2⅛ yards of main print for Plain Square blocks and border
- 2 yards of dark for Rail Fence blocks, Nine Patch blocks, and binding
- 1¼ yards of medium for Rail Fence blocks and Nine Patch blocks
- ⅝ yard of light for Rail Fence blocks
- 5¼ yards of fabric for backing
- 58" x 82" piece of batting

CUTTING

All measurements include ¼"-wide seam allowances. Cut all pieces across the fabric width unless otherwise indicated.

From the light fabric, cut:
- 7 strips, 2½" x width of fabric

From the medium fabric, cut:
- 15 strips, 2½" x width of fabric

From the dark fabric, cut:
- 17 strips, 2½" x width of fabric

From the main print, cut:
- 2 strips, 6½" x 66½", from the lengthwise grain
- 2 strips, 6½" x 54½", from the lengthwise grain
- 7 squares, 6½" x 6½"

PIECING THE BLOCKS

1. Stitch a light strip to a medium strip along one long edge. Stitch a dark strip to the remaining long edge of the medium strip. Press the seams toward the medium strip. Make seven strip sets. From the strip sets, cut 38 segments, 6½" wide, to make the Rail Fence blocks.

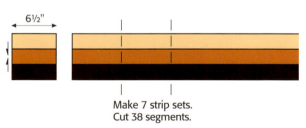

6½"

Make 7 strip sets.
Cut 38 segments.

2. Stitch a medium strip to each side of a dark strip. Press the seams toward the dark strip. Make two strip sets. From the strip sets, cut 32 segments, 2½" wide.

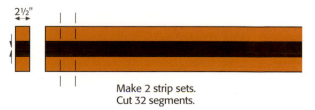

2½"

Make 2 strip sets.
Cut 32 segments.

CAPPUCCINO CROSSROADS

FINISHED QUILT SIZE: 54" x 78" ♦ FINISHED BLOCK SIZE: 6"

3. Sew a dark strip to each side of a medium strip. Press the seams toward the dark strips. Make four strip sets. From the strip sets, cut 64 segments, 2½" wide.

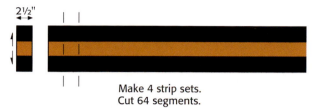

Make 4 strip sets.
Cut 64 segments.

4. Stitch one segment from step 2 and two segments from step 3 together as shown to make a Nine Patch block. Press the seams away from the center segment. Make 32.

Make 32.

ASSEMBLING THE QUILT TOP

1. Arrange the Plain Square blocks, the Rail Fence blocks, and the Nine Patch blocks into rows as shown, paying careful attention to the orientation of the Rail Fence blocks. Stitch the blocks in each row together. Four different row arrangements are repeated to complete the overall design. Make the number indicated for each row arrangement.

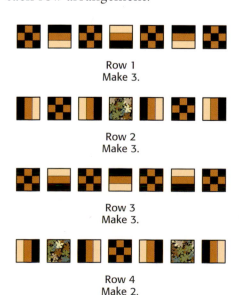

Row 1
Make 3.

Row 2
Make 3.

Row 3
Make 3.

Row 4
Make 2.

2. Follow the quilt assembly diagram to arrange the block rows in the order shown. Stitch the rows together. Sew the 6½" x 66½" main print strips to the sides of the quilt top. Sew the 6½" x 54½" main print strips to the top and bottom edges of the quilt top.

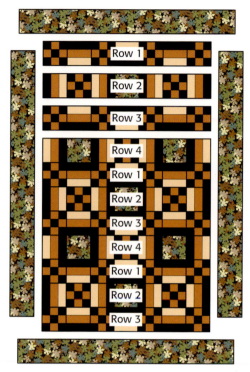

Quilt Assembly Diagram

FINISHING

Refer to "Finishing Touches" on pages 20–23.

1. Layer the quilt top with batting and backing; baste.

2. Quilt as desired.

3. Refer to "Painless Mitered Binding" on page 21 to cut the desired width strips from the remaining dark fabric and bind the quilt.

4. Document your quilt by attaching a label to the back.

BASIC QUILTMAKING SKILLS and thought-ful fabric selection are all you need to make this queen-size beauty that feels as warm as it looks. A pieced dog-tooth inner border frames the quilt and adds interest to its design.

SKILL LEVEL:

Half-Square
Triangle Block

Broken Staircase Blocks

MAIN INGREDIENTS

Yardage is based on 42"-wide fabric.

♦ 4½ yards of main print for Half-Square Triangle blocks and outer border
♦ 2½ yards of black for Broken Staircase blocks, inner border, and binding
♦ 2 yards of brown for Broken Staircase blocks and pieced middle border
♦ 1¾ yards of dark gold for Half-Square Triangle blocks
♦ 1½ yards of medium gold for Broken Staircase blocks
♦ 1½ yards of light gold for Broken Staircase blocks and pieced middle border
♦ ⅝ yard *total* of assorted reds for Broken Staircase blocks
♦ 9 yards of fabric for backing
♦ 96" x 114" piece of batting

CUTTING

All measurements include ¼"-wide seam allowances. Cut all pieces across the fabric width unless otherwise indicated.

From the dark gold, cut:
♦ 20 squares, 9⅞" x 9⅞"

From the main print, cut:
♦ 4 strips, 6" x 112", from the lengthwise grain
♦ 20 squares, 9⅞" x 9⅞"

From the black, cut:
♦ 22 strips, 2" x width of fabric
♦ 2 squares, 2⅜" x 2⅜"; cut each square in half once diagonally to yield 4 half-square triangles

From the light gold, cut:
♦ 3 strips, 2" x width of fabric
♦ 16 squares, 3½" x 3½"
♦ 13 squares, 7¼" x 7¼"; cut each square in half twice diagonally to yield 52 quarter-square triangles. You will use 50 and have 2 left over.
♦ 2 squares, 8⅜" x 8⅜"; cut each square in half once diagonally to yield 4 half-square triangles

From the medium gold, cut:
♦ 10 strips, 2" x width of fabric
♦ 80 squares, 3½" x 3½"

From the brown, cut:
♦ 9 strips, 2" x width of fabric
♦ 64 squares, 3½" x 3½"
♦ 14 squares, 7¼" x 7¼"; cut each square in half twice diagonally to yield 56 quarter-square triangles. You will use 54 and have 2 left over.

From the assorted reds, cut:
♦ 9 strips, 2" x width of fabric

CARAMEL LATTE

Finished quilt size: 92" x 110" ♦ Finished block size: 9"

PIECING THE BLOCKS

1. To make the Half-Square Triangle blocks, draw a diagonal line from corner to corner on the wrong side of each dark gold square. Place each dark gold square on top of a main print square, right sides together. Sew ¼" from both sides of the drawn lines. Cut the squares in half on the drawn lines. Open each half-square triangle and press the seam toward the main print fabric. Make 40.

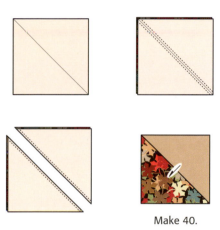

Make 40.

2. To make the Broken Staircase blocks, begin by making the four-patch units for each of the three block color combinations. To construct a four-patch unit, stitch 2"-wide strips together along the long edges to make the strip sets shown below and at right. Make the number of strip sets shown for each color combination. Press the seams toward the black and red strips. Cut each strip set into the number of 2"-wide segments indicated, and then stitch two segments together as shown. Make the number of four-patch units shown for each color combination.

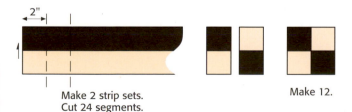

Make 2 strip sets.
Cut 24 segments.

Make 12.

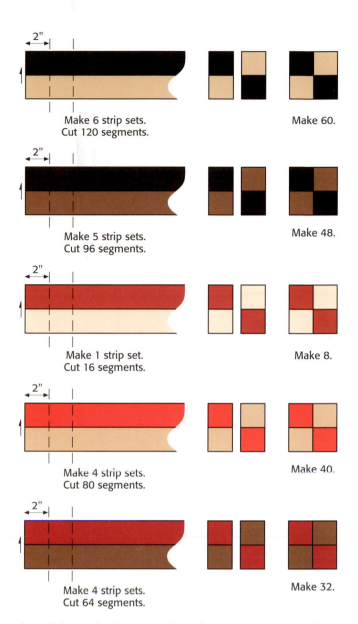

Make 6 strip sets.
Cut 120 segments.

Make 60.

Make 5 strip sets.
Cut 96 segments.

Make 48.

Make 1 strip set.
Cut 16 segments.

Make 8.

Make 4 strip sets.
Cut 80 segments.

Make 40.

Make 4 strip sets.
Cut 64 segments.

Make 32.

3. Stitch the four-patch units and corresponding color 3½" squares together as shown to make the Broken Staircase blocks. Make the number indicated for each color combination.

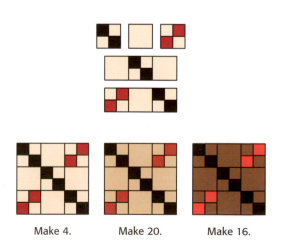

Make 4.   Make 20.   Make 16.

ASSEMBLING THE QUILT TOP

1. Arrange the Half-Square Triangle blocks and Broken Staircase blocks into vertical rows as shown. For a quilt this large, I find it helpful to organize the quilt into more manageable units by assembling the quilt top in quarter sections. For each quarter, stitch the blocks in each row together, then sew the rows together. Sew the quarters together.

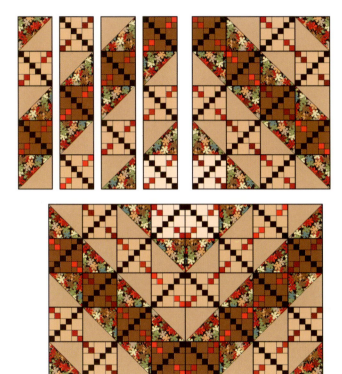

2. To make the inner borders, refer to "Borders" on page 19 to stitch the remaining black 2"-wide strips together to make two strips, 2" x 72½", for the top and bottom borders, and two strips, 2" x 90½", for the side borders.

3. Refer to the quilt assembly diagram to stitch the top and bottom inner border strips to the top and bottom edges of the quilt top. Press the seams toward the borders. Sew a black half-square triangle to each end of the side inner border strips as shown. Stitch the long edge of the strips to the sides of the quilt top. Press the seams toward the borders.

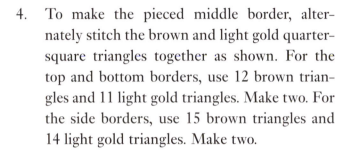

4. To make the pieced middle border, alternately stitch the brown and light gold quarter-square triangles together as shown. For the top and bottom borders, use 12 brown triangles and 11 light gold triangles. Make two. For the side borders, use 15 brown triangles and 14 light gold triangles. Make two.

Top and Bottom Pieced Middle Borders
Make 2.

Side Pieced Middle Borders
Make 2.

5. Refer to the quilt assembly diagram to stitch the top and bottom middle border strips to the top and bottom edges of the quilt top, positioning the strips so the brown triangles are next to the inner borders. Stitch the side middle border strips to the sides of the quilt top. Stitch a light gold half-square triangle to each corner to square up the quilt top.

TIP: Quarter-square triangles can be a little tricky to sew accurately when they are aligned in opposing directions, as they are in the pieced border. When properly aligned for sewing, the ends of the triangles hang over each other, making little "dog ears."

To assist in piecing these triangles, you could purchase an acrylic point-trimming tool available at most quilt stores. This eliminates the "dog ears" and gives you a straight edge for matching. Or, you can locate the exact points for aligning the triangles by marking the seam allowances on the triangles with a pencil. The point where the lines intersect is the point that must be matched with the adjoining triangle when piecing. Mark two triangles in this manner, and then use them as a guide for marking the alignment dots on the remaining triangles.

Align the dots and sew from edge to edge, through the dots, to join the pieces. The sewing line should pass through the small notch where the pieces overlap.

6. Refer to "Borders" on page 19 to measure the quilt top for the top and bottom outer borders. Cut two of the main print 6" x 112" strips to the length measured; stitch the strips to the top and bottom edges of the quilt top. Repeat with the remaining strips for the side outer borders.

Quilt Assembly Diagram

FINISHING

Refer to "Finishing Touches" on pages 20–23.

1. Layer the quilt top with batting and backing; baste.

2. Quilt as desired.

3. Refer to "Painless Mitered Binding" on page 21 to cut the desired width strips from the remaining black fabric and bind the quilt.

4. Document your quilt by attaching a label to the back.

Freeze-Dried Crystals

HAVE YOU EVER wanted to make a Feathered Star block but found it too intimidating to attempt? This block masquerades as a feathered star but has fewer pieces and is much easier to construct. Don't you agree it also would be beautiful in icy blues and silver, or how about a palette of holiday fabrics for a blend of Christmas crystals? Whichever you choose, this table topper is a real dazzler.

SKILL LEVEL:

Crystal Block

MAIN INGREDIENTS

Yardage is based on 42"-wide fabric.

- ♦ ½ yard *each* of 7 assorted medium browns for block backgrounds
- ♦ Fat quarters or ¼ yard *each* of 7 assorted dark browns for crystals
- ♦ 1¼ yards of dark brown for outer border
- ♦ ⅜ yard of medium brown for inner border
- ♦ 3½ yards of fabric for backing
- ♦ ⅝ yard of fabric for binding
- ♦ 58" x 67" piece of batting
- ♦ Chalk marker or water-soluble pen

CUTTING

All measurements include ¼"-wide seam allowances. Cut all pieces across the fabric width unless otherwise indicated.

From *each* dark brown for crystals, cut:
- ♦ 1 square, 5½" x 5½" (A)
- ♦ 4 squares, 3¾" x 3¾"; cut each square in half twice diagonally to yield 16 quarter-square triangles (B)
- ♦ 8 rectangles, 1¾" x 3" (C)

From *each* medium brown for block backgrounds, cut:
- ♦ 1 square, 8⅜" x 8⅜"; cut the square in half twice diagonally to yield 4 quarter-square triangles (D)
- ♦ 2 squares, 4½" x 4½"; cut each square in half once diagonally to yield 4 half-square triangles (E)
- ♦ 4 squares, 3" x 3" (F)
- ♦ 2 squares, 3¾" x 3¾"; cut each square in half twice diagonally to yield 8 quarter-square triangles (G)
- ♦ 8 squares, 2⅛" x 2⅛"; cut each square in half once diagonally to yield 16 half-square triangles (H)
- ♦ 16 squares, 1¾" x 1¾" (I)

From *each* of four of the medium browns for block backgrounds, cut:
- ♦ 1 rectangle, 7⅝" x 14¾" (J)

From the medium brown for inner border, cut:
- ♦ 5 strips, 1½" x width of fabric; crosscut the strips into:
  2 strips, 1½" x 15½"
  2 strips, 1½" x 30½"
  4 strips, 1½" x 20"

From the dark brown for outer border, cut:
- ♦ 2 strips, 5" x 15½", from the lengthwise grain
- ♦ 4 strips, 5" x 31", from the lengthwise grain
- ♦ 2 strips, 5" x 37½", from the lengthwise grain

From the binding fabric, cut:
- ♦ 6 strips, 2⅛" x width of fabric

FREEZE-DRIED CRYSTALS

Finished quilt size: 53¾" x 62¾" ♦ Finished block size: 14¼"

PIECING THE BLOCKS

NOTE: *Use the same color crystal pieces (A–C) and the same color background pieces (D–I) when piecing each block.*

1. Place an I square on one end of a C rectangle, right sides together. Stitch from corner to corner in the direction shown. Press the lower portion of the square to the right side, then fold it back and trim ¼" from the seam. Stitch an I square to the opposite end of the rectangle in the same manner. Press the upper portion of the square to the right side, then fold it back and trim ¼" from the seam. Make four units.

Make 4.

2. Repeat step 1, stitching the squares to the rectangle in the opposite direction to make a mirror-image unit. Make four units.

Make 4.

3. Stitch the units from steps 1 and 2 to the sides of the F squares as shown. Make four units.

4. Sew the short side of a B triangle to each short side of the G triangles. Refer to the tip on page 35 for help in aligning the triangles. Sew an H triangle to the short sides of the B triangles as shown. Make eight units.

Make 8.

5. Stitch one unit from step 3 and two units from step 4 together as shown. Make four units.

Make 4.

6. Arrange the units from step 5, the A square, and the D and E triangles into diagonal rows as shown. Stitch the pieces in each row together, then stitch the rows together, adding the E triangles last.

7. Repeat steps 1–6 to make a total of 7 Crystal blocks.

ASSEMBLING THE QUILT TOP

1. Arrange the J rectangles and the blocks into three vertical rows as shown. Sew the pieces in each row together, and then sew the rows together.

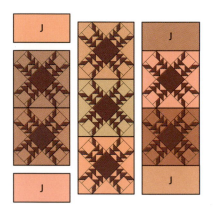

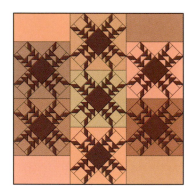

2. Using a chalk marker or water-soluble pen, mark eight small dots ¼" from the edge where shown. Align the ¼" line of a rotary ruler with the dots and cut along the straight edge to trim away the corners. *Do not cut from dot to dot; be sure to cut ¼" beyond the dots.*

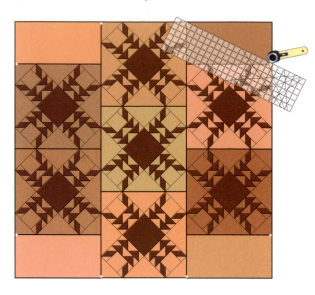

3. Stitch the 1½" x 15½" strips to the top and bottom edges of the quilt top. Stitch the 1½" x 30" strips to the quilt sides. Press the seams toward the strips. The strips are slightly longer than necessary in order to compensate for variations in sewing techniques. When sewing the strips to the quilt top, avoid stretching either the blocks or the strip. This will help ensure the edges do not become wavy. Align the long edge of a rotary ruler with the angled edge of the quilt top as shown and trim the corners of the strips. Add the 1½" x 20" strips to the angled sides, and repeat the trimming process.

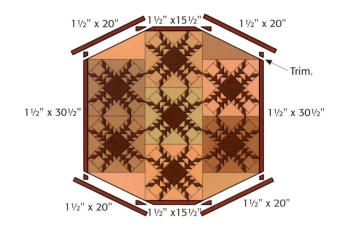

4. Repeat step 3 with the 5"-wide dark brown outer border strips, stitching the strips to the quilt top in the order shown.

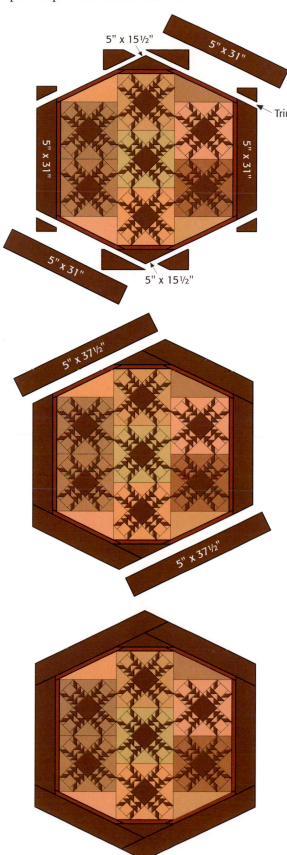

FINISHING

Refer to "Finishing Touches" on pages 20–23.

1. Layer the quilt top with backing and batting; baste.

2. Quilt as desired.

3. Stitch the binding strips together to make one long strip, using diagonal seams to join the strips. Press the strip in half, wrong sides together. Stitch the binding to the edge of the quilt, mitering the corners as shown. Fold the binding to the back of the quilt and hand stitch it in place, mitering the corners.

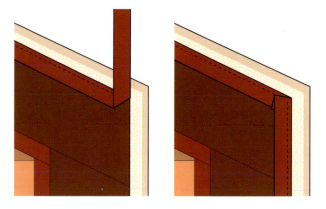

4. Document your quilt by attaching a label to the back.

DOUBLE-SHOT MOCHA CHEESECAKE

Oh, so rich and creamy! This decadent treat is for true chocolate and coffee lovers.

CRUST

  1¾ cups chocolate cookie crumbs
  ¼ cup butter, melted
  3 tablespoons granulated sugar

FILLING

  2 tablespoons water
  2 tablespoons instant coffee crystals
  1 cup semi-sweet chocolate morsels
  ¼ cup coffee liqueur
  3 (8 ounce) packages cream cheese
  1¼ cups granulated sugar
  3 tablespoons all-purpose flour
  1 teaspoon vanilla
  3 eggs
  3 tablespoons milk

1. Prepare the crust: Mix the cookie crumbs, melted butter, and 3 tablespoons sugar. Press into the bottom and along the sides of an ungreased 9" springform pan. Chill the crust while you continue with the recipe.

2. Prepare the filling: In a small saucepan, melt the chocolate morsels in the water and add the coffee crystals. Cool; then add coffee liqueur. **Caution:** *Do not heat liqueur in a saucepan. Be sure the filling has cooled before adding the liqueur.*

3. In another bowl, mix the cream cheese, sugar and flour. Add the vanilla, eggs, milk, and chocolate mixture.

4. Pour the filling mixture into a chilled cookie crust. Bake at 375° for 45 minutes. Leave the cake in the oven with the heat turned off and the door ajar for 45 minutes. Remove from the oven; allow to cool for 45 minutes, and then remove the sides of the pan. Chill at least 4 hours before serving. *Serving option:* Top with fresh raspberries or strawberries.

Mocha Chocolate-Cherry Chewies

These chewy cookies will please your palate with a tasty blend of chocolate, cherries, and just a hint of coffee.

1¾ cups flour
1 teaspoon baking soda
½ teaspoon salt
1 tablespoon instant coffee crystals
1 tablespoon water
¾ cup (1½ sticks) butter
1 cup brown sugar
½ cup granulated sugar
2 eggs
1 teaspoon vanilla
2¼ cups oatmeal
1 cup chocolate chips
½ cup chopped dried cherries

1. In a large bowl combine the flour, baking soda, and salt.

2. Dissolve the coffee crystals in the water.

3. Cream together the butter, sugars, eggs, and vanilla. Add the coffee mixture.

4. Gradually add the oatmeal and dry mixture to the creamed mixture, mixing thoroughly.

5. Stir in the chocolate chips and dried cherries.

6. Drop by rounded teaspoonfuls onto a greased baking sheet.

7. Bake at 375° for 8 to 10 minutes or until golden brown.

8. Cool on a wire rack.

(YIELDS 3½ TO 4 DOZEN)

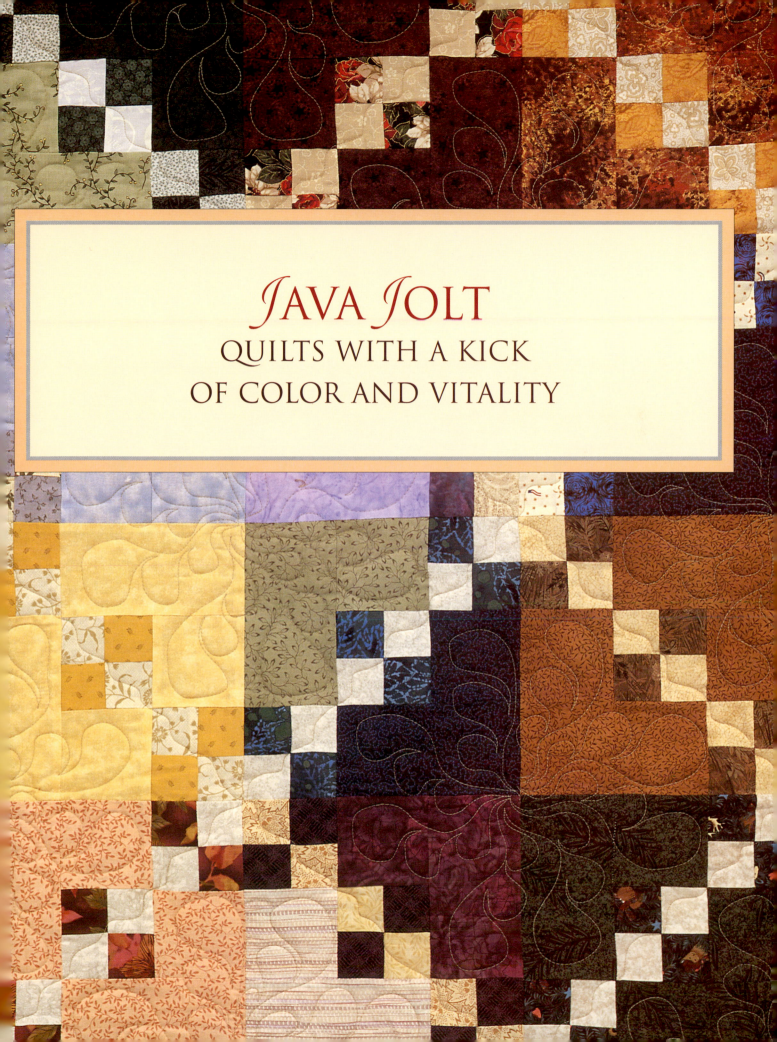

JAVA JOLT
QUILTS WITH A KICK
OF COLOR AND VITALITY

ESPRESSO TO GO

Easy-to-make stars and simple pieced borders combine for a winning combination in this small quilt.

SKILL LEVEL:

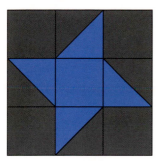

Star Block

MAIN INGREDIENTS

Yardage is based on 42"-wide fabric.

- 2 yards of main print for outer border
- Fat quarters or ¼ yard *each* of 8 assorted bright fabrics for stars and checkerboard border
- 1⅛ yards of black for block backgrounds and sashing
- 3½ yards of fabric for backing
- ¾ yard of fabric for binding
- 55" x 67" piece of batting

CUTTING

All measurements include ¼"-wide seam allowances. Cut all pieces across the fabric width unless otherwise specified.

From *each* of five of the assorted bright fabrics, cut:

- 2 squares, 3⅞" x 3⅞"; cut each square in half once diagonally to yield 4 half-square triangles
- 1 square, 3½" x 3½"

From the remainder of the 8 assorted bright fabrics, cut a *total* of:

- 104 squares, 3½" x 3½"

From the black, cut:

- 10 squares, 3⅞" x 3⅞"; cut each square in half once diagonally to yield 20 half-square triangles
- 20 squares, 3½" x 3½"
- 6 rectangles, 3½" x 9½"
- 2 squares, 9½" x 9½"
- 4 strips, 3½" x 27½"

From the main print, cut:

- 2 strips, 6½" x 39½", from the lengthwise grain
- 2 strips, 6½" x 63½", from the lengthwise grain

PIECING THE BLOCKS

1. Sew a black half-square triangle to each bright half-square triangle as shown. Make 20 half-square triangle units.

Make 20.

2. Arrange four half-square triangle units of the same color, four black 3½" squares, and the matching bright 3½" square into three horizontal rows as shown. Stitch the pieces in each row together, and then stitch the rows together. Make five Star blocks.

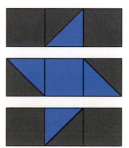 

Make 5.

ESPRESSO TO GO

FINISHED QUILT SIZE: 51" x 63" ♦ FINISHED BLOCK SIZE: 9"

ASSEMBLING THE QUILT TOP

1. Alternately stitch three black 3½" x 9½" sashing rectangles and two Star blocks together as shown. Press the seams toward the sashing. Make two rows.

Make 2.

2. Stitch a black 9½" x 9½" square to each side of the remaining Star block. Press the seams toward the black squares. Make one row.

Make 1.

3. Alternately arrange the three black 3½" x 27½" sashing strips and the block rows from steps 1 and 2 as shown, beginning and ending with a sashing strip. Stitch the sashing strips and block rows together. Press the seams toward the sashing strips.

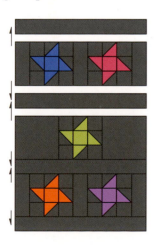

4. To make the inner top and bottom borders, randomly select nine bright 3½" squares and stitch them into a horizontal row. Make four rows. Stitch two rows together as shown. Make two. Make the inner side borders in the same manner, using 17 bright 3½" squares in each row. Make two.

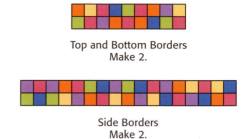

Top and Bottom Borders
Make 2.

Side Borders
Make 2.

5. Refer to the quilt assembly diagram to stitch the inner top and bottom borders to the top and bottom edges of the quilt top. Stitch the inner side borders to the quilt sides. Stitch the main print 6½" x 39½" strips to the top and bottom edges of the quilt top, and then stitch the 6½" x 63½" strips to the quilt sides.

Quilt Assembly Diagram

FINISHING

Refer to "Finishing Touches" on pages 20–23.

1. Layer the quilt top with batting and backing; baste.

2. Quilt as desired.

3. Refer to "Painless Mitered Binding" on page 21 to cut the desired width strips from the binding fabric and bind the quilt.

4. Document your quilt by attaching a label to the back.

HEARTY BLEND

THIS QUILT WILL steal your heart away. The design is created with the basic and versatile Shaded Four Patch block. Don't you agree this would be a great quilt to give as a wedding or anniversary gift?

SKILL LEVEL:

Shaded Four Patch Block

MAIN INGREDIENTS

Yardage is based on 42"-wide fabric.

♦ 3 yards *total* of assorted reds for blocks and sashing cornerstones
♦ 2⅜ yards of deep red for border
♦ 2 yards of light pink for sashing strips
♦ 1½ yards *total* of assorted lights for block backgrounds
♦ 4¾ yards of fabric for backing
♦ ¾ yard of fabric for binding
♦ 71" x 79" piece of batting

CUTTING

All measurements include ¼"-wide seam allowances. Cut all pieces across the fabric width unless otherwise indicated.

From the assorted lights, cut:

♦ 180 squares, 2⅞" x 2⅞"; cut each square in half once diagonally to yield 360 half-square triangles

From the assorted reds, cut:

♦ 188 squares, 2½" x 2½"
♦ 90 squares, 4⅞" x 4⅞"; cut each square in half once diagonally to yield 180 half-square triangles

From the light pink, cut:

♦ 6 rectangles, 2½" x 16½", from the lengthwise grain
♦ 4 strips, 2½" x 60½", from the lengthwise grain

From the deep red, cut:

♦ 2 strips, 6" x 56½", from the lengthwise grain
♦ 2 strips, 6" x 75½", from the lengthwise grain

PIECING THE BLOCKS

1. To make the blocks, stitch a light half-square triangle to two adjacent sides of each red 2½" square as shown to make a pieced triangle.

2. Sew a red half-square triangle to each pieced triangle to complete the blocks. Make 180.

Make 180.

HEARTY BLEND

FINISHED QUILT SIZE: 67" x 75" ♦ FINISHED BLOCK SIZE: 4"

ASSEMBLING THE QUILT TOP

1. Stitch four blocks together as shown to make row A. Make 24 rows. Stitch four blocks together as shown to make row B. Make 21 rows.

Row A
Make 24.

Row B
Make 21.

2. Stitch together eight of row A and seven of row B, alternating rows. Begin and end with row A. Make three vertical panels.

Row A

Row B

Make 3.

3. Refer to the quilt assembly diagram to alternately stitch the light pink 2½" x 60½" strips and panels together, beginning and ending with a strip.

4. To make the pieced top and bottom sashing strips, alternately stitch four red 2½" squares and three light pink 2½" x 16½" rectangles together, beginning and ending with a square. Make two.

Make 2.

5. Refer to the quilt assembly diagram to stitch a pieced sashing strip to the top and bottom edges of the quilt top.

6. Stitch the deep red 6" x 56½" strips to the top and bottom edges of the quilt top. Stitch the 6" x 75½" strips to the quilt sides.

Quilt Assembly Diagram

FINISHING

Refer to "Finishing Touches" on pages 20–23.

1. Layer the quilt top with batting and backing; baste.

2. Quilt as desired.

3. Refer to "Painless Mitered Binding" on page 21 to cut the desired width strips from the binding fabric and bind the quilt.

4. Document your quilt by attaching a label to the back.

HEARTY BLEND LITE

This heart-warming wall hanging is a great project for novice quilters eager to tackle triangles or for quilters ready to learn appliqué. The block that creates this design is the same Shaded Four Patch block used to make "Hearty Blend" on page 50.

SKILL LEVEL:

Shaded Four Patch Block

MAIN INGREDIENTS

Yardage is based on 42"-wide fabric.

- 1 yard *total* of assorted reds for pieced blocks and appliqués
- ⅜ yard *total* of assorted lights for pieced block backgrounds
- 8½" x 8½" square of light solid for appliqué block background
- 1⅛ yards of fabric for backing
- ½ yard of red for binding
- 32" x 32" square of batting
- Fusible web or freezer paper, depending on the appliqué method used

CUTTING

All measurements include ¼"-wide seam allowances. Cut all pieces across the fabric width unless otherwise indicated.

From the assorted reds, cut:
- 36 squares, 2½" x 2½"
- 18 squares, 4⅞" x 4⅞"; cut each square in half once diagonally to yield 36 half-square triangles
- 5 squares, 6⅞" x 6⅞"; cut each square in half twice diagonally to yield 20 quarter-square triangles

From the assorted lights, cut:
- 36 squares, 2⅞" x 2⅞"; cut each square in half once diagonally to yield 72 half-square triangles

PIECING THE BLOCKS

1. Stitch a light half-square triangle to two adjacent sides of each red 2½" square as shown to make a pieced triangle.

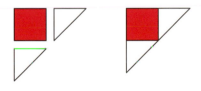

2. Sew a red half-square triangle to each pieced triangle to complete the pieced blocks. Make 36.

Make 36.

HEARTY BLEND LITE

FINISHED QUILT SIZE: 28⅛" x 28⅛" ♦ FINISHED BLOCK SIZE: 4"

ASSEMBLING THE QUILT TOP

1. Refer to the quilt assembly diagram to stitch the pieced blocks, the 8½" x 8½" light square, and the assorted red quarter-square triangles into rows as shown. Stitch the pieces in each row together. Stitch the rows together.

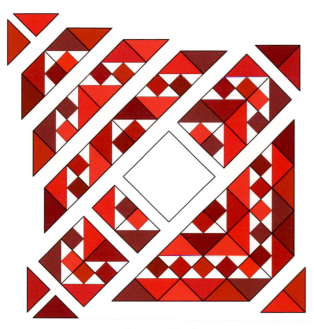

Quilt Assembly Diagram

2. Use the pattern at right and refer to "Appliqué Techniques" on page 15 to make four heart appliqués from one of the remaining assorted red fabrics, using your favorite appliqué method. Center the hearts on the quilt top center square as shown and appliqué them in place.

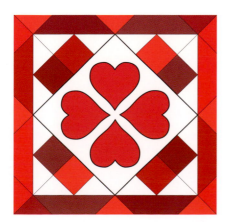

FINISHING

Refer to "Finishing Touches" on pages 20–23.

1. Layer the quilt top with batting and backing; baste.

2. Quilt as desired.

3. Refer to "Painless Mitered Binding" on page 21 to cut the desired width strips from the red binding fabric and bind the quilt.

4. Document your quilt by attaching a label to the back.

Heart Appliqué Pattern

THE SMALL, LIGHT chain of squares that swirls across the surface of this "sweet" quilt represents white sugar cubes. This is a great utility quilt and a perfect project for using up scraps.

SKILL LEVEL:

Sugar Cube Blocks

MAIN INGREDIENTS

Yardage is based on 42"-wide fabric.

- 2¼ yards *total* of assorted darks for blocks
- 1½ yards *total* of assorted mediums for blocks
- 1 yard *total* of assorted lights for blocks
- 3½ yards of fabric for backing
- ¾ yard of fabric for binding
- 58" x 76" piece of batting

CUTTING

All measurements include ¼"-wide seam allowances. Cut all pieces across the width of the fabric unless otherwise indicated.

NOTE: *When working with scraps, I prefer to cut the pieces for one block and then stack the pieces together, set them aside, and cut the next block. I repeat this process until I've cut the pieces for each of the blocks required. This helps keep me organized and aids in balancing colors throughout the quilt. Because there are three different value combinations, be sure to label each stack with the color-variation letter as you set it aside.*

For Color-variation A
(repeat to cut pieces for 28 blocks)

From one light, cut:
- 6 squares, 2" x 2"

From one medium, cut:
- 6 squares, 2" x 2"

From one dark, cut:
- 2 squares, 3½" x 3½"
- 2 rectangles, 3½" x 6½"

For Color-variation B
(repeat to cut pieces for 8 blocks)

From one light, cut:
- 6 squares, 2" x 2"

From one medium, cut:
- 6 squares, 2" x 2"

From a different medium, cut:
- 2 squares, 3½" x 3½"
- 2 rectangles, 3½" x 6½"

For Color-variation C
(repeat to cut pieces for 12 blocks)

From one light, cut:
- 6 squares, 2" x 2"

From one medium, cut:
- 1 square, 3½" x 3½"
- 1 rectangle, 3½" x 6½"

From one dark, cut:
- 1 square, 3½" x 3½"
- 1 rectangle, 3½" x 6½"

From a different dark, cut:
- 6 squares, 2" x 2"

ONE LUMP OR TWO?

PIECING THE BLOCKS

1. Using the pieces in one color-variation A stack, sew each light 2" square to the medium 2" squares. Stitch the units together in pairs as shown to make three four-patch units.

Make 3.

2. Sew the dark 3½" squares to two of the four-patch units as shown, then stitch the units together. Be sure the four-patch units are oriented in the correct direction so that the chain of light squares runs diagonally across the block.

3. Stitch a dark rectangle to the top of the unit from step 2 as shown.

4. Stitch the remaining dark rectangle to the remaining four-patch unit as shown.

5. Sew the four-patch unit from step 4 to the right-hand side of the unit from step 3 to complete the block.

Color-variation A

6. Repeat steps 1–5 with the remaining color-variation A stacks. Make a total of 28 color-variation A blocks.

7. Using the pieces in one block B stack, repeat step 1 to make the four-patch units. Repeat steps 2–5 using the medium 3½" squares and 3½" x 6½" rectangles. Repeat with the remaining color-variation B stacks. Make a total of eight color-variation B blocks.

Color-variation B
Make 8.

8. Using the pieces in one color-variation C stack, repeat step 1 to make the four-patch units, using the dark and light squares. Repeat steps 2–5 using the medium and dark 3½" squares and 3½" x 6½" rectangles to complete the block as shown. Repeat with the remaining color-variation C stacks. Make a total of 12 color-variation C blocks.

Color-variation C
Make 12.

ASSEMBLING THE QUILT TOP

ARRANGE blocks A, B, and C into horizontal rows, rotating the blocks as shown. For a quilt this large, I find it helpful to organize the quilt into more manageable units by assembling the quilt top in quarter sections. For each quarter, stitch the blocks in each row together, then sew the rows together. Sew the quarters together.

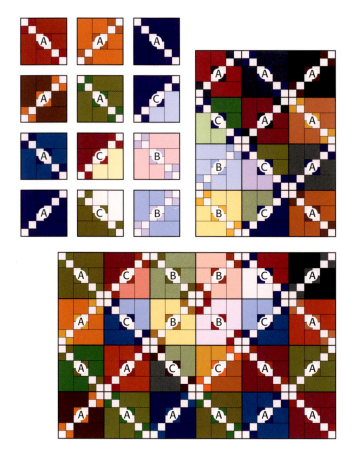

FINISHING

Refer to "Finishing Touches" on pages 20–23.

1. Layer the quilt top with batting and backing; baste.

2. Quilt as desired.

3. Refer to "Painless Mitered Binding" on page 21 to cut the desired width strips from the binding fabric and bind the quilt.

4. Document your quilt by attaching a label to the back.

CARAMEL LATTE CAKE

Whipped topping is the perfect partner for this yummy dessert.

1 package chocolate cake mix
3 eggs
⅓ cup vegetable oil
½ cup coffee liqueur
3 tablespoons instant coffee crystals, dissolved in
    ¾ cup water (or substitute ¾ cup strong
    brewed coffee)
⅔ cup sweetened condensed milk
⅔ cup caramel ice cream topping
12 ounces non-dairy whipped topping
¼ cup finely chopped hazelnuts or pecans

1. Preheat the oven to 350°. Lightly grease and flour a 9" x 13" baking pan.

2. Combine the cake mix, eggs, oil, coffee liqueur, and coffee mixture in a large bowl. Beat well. Pour into a prepared pan.

3. Bake for 28 to 30 minutes or until the cake springs back when touched. Cool slightly. Then poke holes in the cake with a round dowel or the handle of a wooden spoon. Pour sweetened condensed milk over the warm cake; then pour the caramel ice cream topping over the cake. Let cool.

4. Top with whipped topping and nuts.

CUPS AND SAUCERS TABLE RUNNER

When I stumbled across this coffee-flavored fabric, I knew in an instant it called out for the traditional Cups and Saucers block. Select a fabric that coordinates with your kitchen—perhaps a fruit motif, vegetables, or country chickens—if you find something that is more to your liking. Another option would be to give your table runner a seasonal flavor for an upcoming holiday or special time of the year.

Skill level:

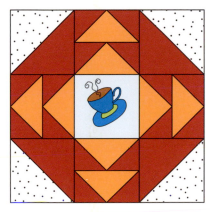

Cups and Saucers Block

MAIN INGREDIENTS

Yardage is based on 42"-wide fabric.

- ⅝ yard of main print for blocks and outer border
- ½ yard of dark red for blocks
- ¼ yard of gold for blocks
- ¼ yard of light for block backgrounds
- ¼ yard of black for inner border and binding
- 1⅝ yards of fabric for backing
- 25" x 49" piece of batting

CUTTING

All measurements include ¼"-wide seam allowances. Cut all pieces across the fabric width unless otherwise indicated.

From the light, cut:
- 6 squares, 4⅞" x 4⅞"; cut each square in half once diagonally to yield 12 half-square triangles

From the dark red, cut:
- 6 squares, 4⅞" x 4⅞"; cut each square in half once diagonally to yield 12 half-square triangles
- 24 squares, 2⅞" x 2⅞"; cut each square in half once diagonally to yield 48 half-square triangles

From the gold, cut:
- 6 squares, 5¼" x 5¼"; cut each square in half twice diagonally to yield 24 quarter-square triangles

From the main print, cut:
- 3 squares, 4½" x 4½"
- 2 strips, 4½" x 39½"
- 2 strips, 4½" x 23½"

From the black, cut:
- 2 strips, 2" x 12½"
- 2 strips, 2" x 39½"

PIECING THE BLOCKS

1. Sew a light 4⅞" half-square triangle to each dark red 4⅞" half-square triangle as shown. Make 12 half-square triangle units.

Make 12.

CUPS AND SAUCERS TABLE RUNNER

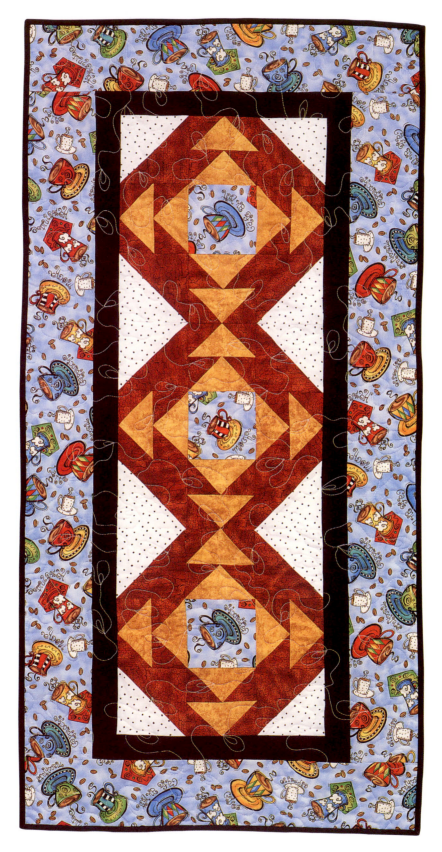

Finished table runner size: 23" x 47" ◆ **Finished block size: 12"**

2. Sew a dark red 2⅞" half-square triangle to the two short edges of each gold quarter-square triangle. Make 24 flying geese units.

Make 24.

3. Stitch the flying geese units together in pairs, orienting the points in the same direction. Make 12 flying geese pairs.

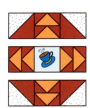

Make 12.

4. Arrange the four half-square triangle units, four flying geese pairs, and one main print 4½" square into rows as shown. Stitch the pieces in each row together, and then stitch the rows together to complete the block. Make three Cups and Saucers blocks.

Make 3.

ASSEMBLING THE TABLE RUNNER TOP

1. Stitch the blocks together as shown.

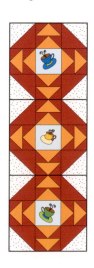

2. Refer to the table runner assembly diagram to stitch the inner and outer borders to the table runner top. Stitch the black 2" x 39½" strips to the sides of the table runner top. Sew the black 2" x 12½" strips to the top and bottom edges of the table runner top. Stitch the main print 4½" x 23½" strips to the top and bottom edges of the table runner top, and then stitch the main print 4½" x 39½" strips to the sides.

Table Runner Assembly Diagram

FINISHING

Refer to "Finishing Touches" on pages 20–23.

1. Layer the table runner top with batting and backing; baste.

2. Quilt as desired.

3. Refer to "Painless Mitered Binding" on page 21 to cut the desired width strips from the remaining black fabric and bind the table runner.

The traditional Cups and Saucers block receives a few minor adjustments to make it just right for place mats that coordinate perfectly with the table runner on page 64. This ensemble is great for everyday use or for giving as a housewarming gift.

SKILL LEVEL:

MAIN INGREDIENTS

Yardage is based on 42"-wide fabric. The yardage given is sufficient for two place mats. Adjust the yardage accordingly if you are making additional place mats.

♦ ⅝ yard of main print for place-mat center and border
♦ ½ yard of dark red for place-mat center
♦ ¼ yard of gold for place-mat center
♦ ¼ yard of light for place-mat center
♦ 1 yard of fabric for backing
♦ ½ yard of black for binding
♦ 1 yard of batting

CUTTING INSTRUCTIONS

All measurements include ¼"-wide seam allowances. Cut all pieces across the fabric width unless otherwise indicated.

From the dark red, cut:
♦ 12 squares, 2⅞" x 2⅞"; cut each square in half once diagonally to yield 24 half-square triangles
♦ 1 square, 5¼" x 5¼"; cut the square in half twice diagonally to yield 4 quarter-square triangles
♦ 8 rectangles, 2½" x 4½"

From the gold, cut:
♦ 3 squares, 5¼" x 5¼"; cut each square in half twice diagonally to yield 12 quarter-square triangles

From the light, cut:
♦ 4 squares, 2⅞" x 2⅞"; cut each square in half once diagonally to yield 8 half-square triangles
♦ 16 squares, 2½" x 2½"

From the main print, cut:
♦ 2 squares, 4½" x 4½"
♦ 4 strips, 2½" x 8½"
♦ 4 strips, 2½" x 20½"

From the backing, cut:
♦ 2 rectangles, 16" x 24"

From the batting, cut:
♦ 2 rectangles, 14" x 22"

CUPS AND SAUCERS PLACE MATS

FINISHED PLACE MAT SIZE: 12" x 20"

ASSEMBLING THE PLACE MATS

1. Sew a dark red 2⅞" half-square triangle to the two short edges of each gold quarter-square triangle. Make 12 flying geese units. In the same manner, sew a light 2⅞" half-square triangle to the two short edges of each dark red quarter-square triangle. Make 4 flying geese units.

Make 12.

Make 4.

2. Align a light 2½" square with one end of a dark red rectangle as shown, right sides together. Sew diagonally across the square from corner to corner. Press the lower portion of the square to the right side, then fold it back and trim ¼" from the seam. Make four units. Repeat to make four additional units, stitching from opposite corners as shown, and pressing the upper portion to the right side.

Make 4.

Make 4.

3. Arrange the light 2½" squares, the main print 4½" squares, and the units from steps 1 and 2 into vertical rows as shown. Sew the pieces in each row together and then sew the rows together. Make two place-mat centers.

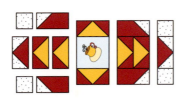

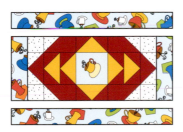

Make 2.

4. Stitch the main print 2½" x 8½" strips to the ends of each place-mat center. Sew the 2½" x 20½" strips to the top and bottom edges of each place-mat center.

FINISHING

Refer to "Finishing Touches" on pages 20–23.

1. Layer each place mat with batting and backing; baste.

2. Quilt as desired.

3. Refer to "Painless Mitered Binding" on page 21 to cut the desired width strips from the black fabric and bind each place mat.

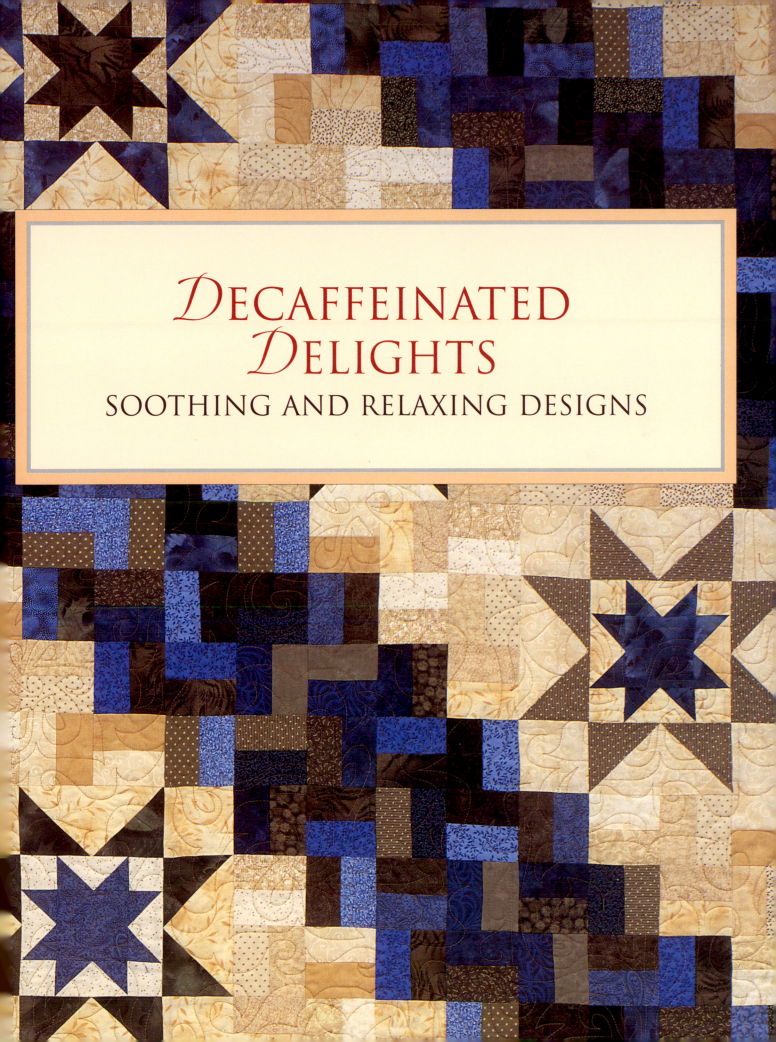

DECAFFEINATED DELIGHTS

SOOTHING AND RELAXING DESIGNS

TOTALLY DECAFFEINATED

A RELAXING PALETTE evokes a peaceful feeling in this generous queen-size quilt. Rising Star blocks appear to float above a seashore of Stacked Logs blocks in dazzling blues, rich greens, and warm, sandy tones.

SKILL LEVEL:

Stacked Logs Block   Rising Star Block

MAIN INGREDIENTS

Yardage is based on 42"-wide fabric.

- 5½ yards *total* or ¼ yard *each* of 22 assorted creams, off-whites, and tans for blocks and flying geese border
- 3½ yards *total* or ¼ yard *each* of 14 assorted dark blues for blocks and flying geese border
- 3½ yards *total* or ¼ yard *each* of 14 assorted dark greens for blocks and flying geese border
- 3¼ yards of main print for outer border
- ¾ yard of dark green for inner border
- 8¾ yards of fabric for backing
- 1¼ yards of fabric for binding
- 102" x 114" piece of batting

CUTTING

All measurements include ¼"-wide seam allowances. Cut all pieces across the fabric width unless otherwise indicated.

NOTE: *Each Rising Star block requires four different fabrics: one dark and one light for the inner star, and*

a different dark and a different light for the outer star. I prefer to cut the pieces for one Rising Star block and then stack the pieces together, set them aside, and cut the next block. I repeat this process until I've cut the pieces for each of the blocks required. This helps keep me organized and aids in balancing colors throughout the quilt. Cut the pieces for the Stacked Logs blocks and borders first and then cut the pieces for the Rising Star blocks from the remaining assorted light and dark fabrics.

For the Stacked Logs Blocks and Borders

From the assorted lights, cut a *total* of:
- 36 strips, 2" x width of fabric
- 66 squares, 3⅞" x 3⅞"; cut each square in half once diagonally to yield 132 half-square triangles

From the assorted darks, cut a *total* of:
- 60 strips, 2" x width of fabric
- 17 squares, 7¼" x 7¼"; cut each square in half twice diagonally to yield 68 quarter-square triangles. You will use 66 and have 2 left over.

From the dark green, cut:
- 10 strips, 2" x width of fabric

From the main print, cut:
- 2 strips, 6" x 87½", from the lengthwise grain
- 2 strips, 6" x 110½", from the lengthwise grain

For the Rising Star Blocks
(repeat to cut pieces for 16 blocks)

From one light, cut:
- 4 squares, 2" x 2"
- 1 square, 4¼" x 4¼"; cut the square in half twice diagonally to yield 4 quarter-square triangles

From one dark, cut:
- 1 square, 3½" x 3½"
- 4 squares, 2⅜" x 2⅜"; cut each square in half once diagonally to yield 8 half-square triangles

TOTALLY DECAFFEINATED

FINISHED QUILT SIZE: 98" x 110" ◆ FINISHED BLOCK SIZE: 12"

From a different light, cut:

- 4 squares, 3½" x 3½"
- 1 square, 7¼" x 7¼"; cut the square in half twice diagonally to yield 4 quarter-square triangles

From a different dark, cut:

- 4 squares, 3⅞" x 3⅞"; cut each square in half once diagonally to yield 8 half-square triangles

PIECING THE BLOCKS

1. To make the Rising Star blocks, using the pieces from one stack, sew a dark 2⅜" half-square triangle to the two short edges of each light 4¼" quarter-square triangle as shown. Make four small flying geese units for the inner star. Repeat with the remaining dark half-square triangles and light quarter-square triangles to make four large flying geese units for the outer star.

Make 4.

Make 4.

2. Arrange the four small flying geese units from step 1, the four light 2" squares, and the dark 3½" square into three vertical rows as shown. Stitch the pieces in each row together and then stitch the rows together to complete the inner star unit.

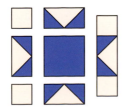

3. Arrange the four large flying geese units from step 1, the four light 3½" squares, and the inner star unit into three vertical rows as shown. Stitch the pieces in each row together and then stitch the rows together to complete the block.

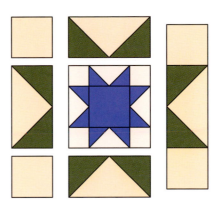

4. Repeat steps 1–3 with each of the remaining stacks to make a total of 16 Rising Star blocks.

5. To make the Stacked Logs blocks, randomly select two different light 2"-wide strips and stitch them together along the long edges to make a strip set. Press the seam to one side. Make 18. Crosscut the strip sets into 192 segments, each 3½" wide.

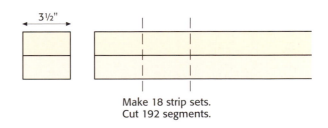

3½"

Make 18 strip sets.
Cut 192 segments.

6. Randomly select two different dark 2"-wide strips and stitch them together along the long edges to make a strip set. Press the seam to one side. Make 30. Crosscut the strip sets into 320 segments, each 3½" wide.

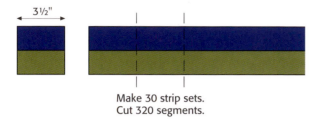

Make 30 strip sets.
Cut 320 segments.

TIP: When choosing fabrics for the strip sets, don't waste time obsessing about which fabrics to pair together. Just grab and go! Once the strips are cut into smaller units, they will blend perfectly, even if two identical pieces end up touching each other after the blocks are sewn together.

7. Arrange ten dark segments and six light segments into four rows of four segments each as shown. Pay close attention to the orientation of each segment. When the segments are oriented in the correct directions, you will not need to match seams within each block or when sewing the blocks to each other. Sew the segments in each row together and then sew the rows together. Make 32 Stacked Logs blocks.

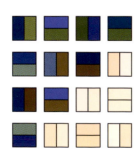 

Make 32.

ASSEMBLING THE QUILT TOP

1. Arrange the Rising Star blocks and Stacked Logs blocks into horizontal rows, rotating the Stacked Logs blocks as shown. For a quilt this large, I find it helpful to organize the quilt into more manageable units by assembling the quilt top in quarter sections. For each quarter, stitch the blocks in each row together, and then sew the rows together. Sew the quarters together.

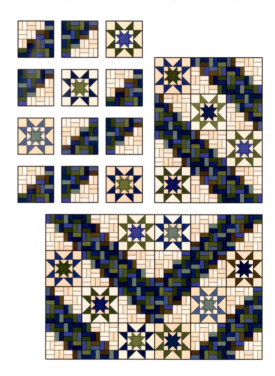

2. To make the inner borders, refer to "Borders" on page 19 to stitch the dark green strips together to make two strips, 2" x 72½", for the top and bottom borders, and two strips, 2" x 99½", for the side borders. Refer to the quilt assembly diagram to stitch the top and bottom borders to the top and bottom edges of the quilt top. Sew the side borders to the sides of the quilt top.

3. To make the flying geese borders, randomly select two light 3⅞" half-square triangles and stitch them to the short sides of each dark 7¼" quarter-square triangle as shown. Make 66 flying geese units.

Make 66.

4. Stitch 33 flying geese units together, orienting the points in the same direction. Make two strips. Refer to the quilt assembly diagram to stitch the strips to the sides of the quilt top.

Make 2.

5. Stitch the main print 6" x 87½" strips to the top and bottom edges of the quilt top, and then stitch the 6" x 110½" strips to the quilt sides.

FINISHING

Refer to "Finishing Touches" on pages 20–23.

1. Layer the quilt top with batting and backing; baste.

2. Quilt as desired.

3. Refer to "Painless Mitered Binding" on page 21 to cut the desired width strips from the binding fabric and bind the quilt.

4. Document your quilt by attaching a label to the back.

Quilt Assembly Diagram

PERCOLATING PINWHEELS

THIS IS A quick and easy project. Traditional Double Pinwheel blocks are paired with smaller Pinwheel blocks in this simple but striking design.

SKILL LEVEL:

Pinwheel Block   Double Pinwheel Block

MAIN INGREDIENTS

Yardage is based on 42"-wide fabric.

- 1⅛ yards of light for blocks, background pieces, and inner border
- 1⅛ yards of main print for Double Pinwheel blocks and outer border
- ¼ yard of dark that coordinates with main print for Double Pinwheel blocks (dark 1)
- ¼ yard of a different dark for Pinwheel blocks (dark 2)
- 1⅜ yards of fabric for backing
- ½ yard of fabric for binding
- 40" x 40" square of batting

CUTTING

All measurements include ¼"-wide seam allowances. Cut all pieces across the fabric width unless otherwise indicated.

From the light, cut:

- 5 squares, 5¼" x 5¼"; cut each square in half twice diagonally to yield 20 quarter-square triangles

- 24 squares, 2⅞" x 2⅞"; cut each square in half once diagonally to yield 48 half-square triangles
- 2 strips, 2½" x 8½" (A)
- 2 strips, 4½" x 12½" (B)
- 6 strips, 2½" x 12½" (C)
- 2 strips, 2½" x 28½" (D)
- 2 strips, 2½" x 32½" (E)

From dark 1, cut:

- 5 squares, 5¼" x 5¼"; cut each square in half twice diagonally to yield 20 quarter-square triangles

From the main print, cut:

- 2 strips, 2½" x 32½", from the lengthwise grain (F)
- 2 strips, 2½" x 36½", from the lengthwise grain (G)
- 10 squares, 4⅞" x 4⅞"; cut each square in half once diagonally to yield 20 half-square triangles

From dark 2, cut:

- 24 squares, 2⅞" x 2⅞"; cut each square in half once diagonally to yield 48 half-square triangles

PIECING THE BLOCKS

1. To make the Double Pinwheel blocks, stitch each light quarter-square triangle to a dark 1 quarter-square triangle to make a quarter-square triangle unit. Sew a main print half-square triangle to each quarter-square triangle unit to make a pieced square. Make 20.

Make 20.

PERCOLATING PINWHEELS

FINISHED QUILT SIZE: 36" x 36"   ♦   FINISHED BLOCK SIZES: DOUBLE PINWHEEL: 8", PINWHEEL: 4"

2. Stitch four pieced squares together as shown to complete the block. Make five.

Make 5.

3. To make the Pinwheel blocks, stitch each light half-square triangle to a dark 2 half-square triangle to make a half-square-triangle unit. Make 48.

Make 48.

4. Stitch four half-square-triangle units together as shown to complete the block. Make 12.

Make 12.

ASSEMBLING THE QUILT TOP

1. Stitch an A strip to the top and bottom edges of one Double Pinwheel block as shown.

2. Stitch three Pinwheel blocks together as shown. Make four Pinwheel strips.

Make 4.

3. Stitch a B strip to the top edge and a C strip to the bottom edge of two of the Pinwheel strips.

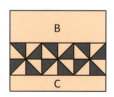

Make 2.

4. Stitch a C strip to the top and bottom edges of the remaining two Pinwheel strips, then sew a Double Pinwheel block to each end as shown.

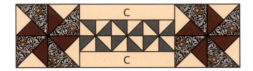

Make 2.

5. Stitch the B/C Pinwheel strips to the sides of the unit from step 1, positioning the strip so the B strips are closest to the unit. Stitch the remaining Pinwheel strips to the top and bottom edges of the unit.

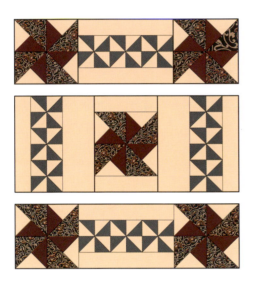

6. Refer to the quilt assembly diagram to stitch the D strips to the top and bottom edges of the quilt top and the E strips to the sides of the quilt top. Repeat to sew the F and G strips to the quilt top.

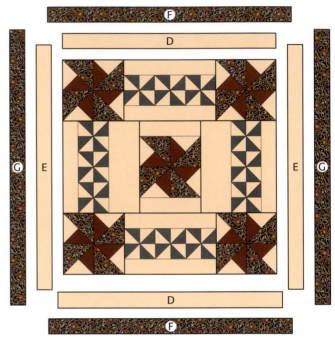

Quilt Assembly Diagram

FINISHING

Refer to "Finishing Touches" on pages 20–23.

1. Layer the quilt top with batting and backing; baste.

2. Quilt as desired.

3. Refer to "Painless Mitered Binding" on page 21 to cut the desired width strips from the binding fabric and bind the quilt.

4. Document your quilt by attaching a label to the back.

Mom's Cinnamon-Pecan Coffee Cake

In addition to her other fine attributes, my mother-in-law, Henrietta Wierzbicki, is an exceptional cook who generously shares her baked goods with friends, neighbors, and church bake sales. This recipe is one of her specialties. It yields two loaves, enough for a family gathering or for sharing with a friend.

COFFEE CAKE

4 cups all-purpose flour
1 cup plus ¼ cup granulated white sugar
1 teaspoon salt
1 cup (2 sticks) butter or margarine
1 envelope active dry yeast
¼ cup warm water (105° to 110°)
1 cup warm milk (105° to 110°)
3 egg yolks, beaten
3 egg whites
1 cup chopped pecans
2 teaspoons ground cinnamon

ICING

1 cup sifted powdered sugar
¼ teaspoon vanilla
Milk

1. In a large bowl, sift together the flour, ¼ cup sugar, and salt. Cut in the butter until the mixture clumps into the size of small peas; set aside.

2. In a small bowl, dissolve the yeast in ¼ cup warm water. Let stand for 5 to 10 minutes to soften. In another small bowl, combine the cup of warm milk with the beaten egg yolks. Stir in the softened yeast.

3. Add the yeast mixture to the flour mixture. Using a wooden spoon, beat the mixture by hand until a soft dough forms. Cover with oiled waxed paper and then plastic wrap and refrigerate overnight.

4. Divide the dough in half. On a lightly floured surface, roll each dough portion into a 9" x 14" rectangle, about ¼" thick.

5. Beat the egg whites with an electric mixer until stiff peaks form. In a small mixing bowl, combine 1 cup sugar, the chopped pecans, and cinnamon. Fold into the beaten egg whites. Spread each rectangle with half the egg white mixture. Starting on a long edge, tightly roll up each rectangle, jelly-roll style. Place the shaped loaves on a greased 15" x 10" x 1" baking sheet. Cover and let rise in a warm place until nearly double in size (about 45 minutes).

6. Bake in a 350° oven for 35 to 40 minutes or until the loaves sound hollow when tapped on top with fingers; cool slightly.

7. Mix the icing ingredients together, adding milk until the icing is smooth and easy to drizzle. Drizzle the icing over the warm coffee cakes.

(YIELDS 2)

SERVICE FOR FOUR

Bright floral prints give this wall hanging the look of fine bone china. Easy appliqué makes the project suitable for all skill levels. This quilt was inspired by the beautiful china painted by my mother, Shirley Sullivan, and my grandmother, Dorothy Reimann. Their works are treasured family heirlooms. Some of their pieces are shown at left.

SKILL LEVEL:

MAIN INGREDIENTS

Yardage is based on 42"-wide fabric.

- ½ yard of floral print for border and coffeepot
- ½ yard *total* of assorted darks for appliqué background squares
- ¼ yard of light for border
- Scraps of four assorted prints for coffee mugs and coffeepot lid, handle, and feet appliqués
- 1 yard of fabric for backing
- ½ yard of fabric for binding
- 27" x 27" square of batting
- Fusible web or freezer paper, depending on the appliqué method used

CUTTING

All measurements include ¼"-wide seam allowances. Cut all pieces across the fabric width unless otherwise indicated.

From the assorted darks, cut:
- 4 squares, 6½" x 6½"
- 4 squares, 6" x 6"

From the light, cut:
- 8 strips, 1¾" x 12½"

From the floral print, cut:
- 4 strips, 3½" x 12½"

ASSEMBLING THE QUILT TOP

1. Sew the dark 6½" squares together as shown to make the quilt-center background.

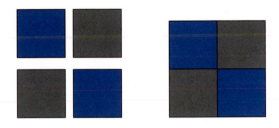

2. Sew a light strip to each long side of a floral print strip to make the border units.

SERVICE FOR FOUR

FINISHED QUILT SIZE: 23" x 23"

3. Stitch a border unit to the top and bottom edges of the quilt-center background. Sew a dark 6" square to the ends of the remaining two border units. Stitch these strips to the sides of the quilt-center background.

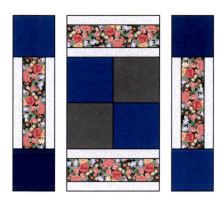

APPLIQUÉING THE QUILT TOP

1. Use the patterns on pages 90–91 and refer to "Appliqué Techniques" on page 15 to make the appliqués. Make one coffeepot appliqué (B) from the floral print. From the assorted prints, make one handle (A), one lid (C), one lid top (D), two coffeepot feet (D), two mugs and two mugs reversed (E).

2. Working in alphabetical order, arrange the coffeepot appliqués (A–D) on the quilt-center background so the coffeepot will be centered when the appliqués are stitched or fused in place. If you are fusing the appliqués in place,

remove the paper backing before arranging the appliqués and then fuse them in place when you are satisfied with the arrangement. If you are hand stitching the appliqués in place, arrange the appliqués and then remove all of the shapes but the handle. Appliqué the handle in place and then work in alphabetical order to replace each shape and appliqué it in place.

3. Appliqué a mug to the center of each border corner square.

FINISHING

Refer to "Finishing Touches" on pages 20–23.

1. Layer the quilt top with batting and backing; baste.

2. Quilt as desired.

3. Refer to "Painless Mitered Binding" on page 21 to cut the desired width strips from the binding fabric and bind the quilt.

4. Document your quilt by attaching a label to the back.

Appliqué Pattern

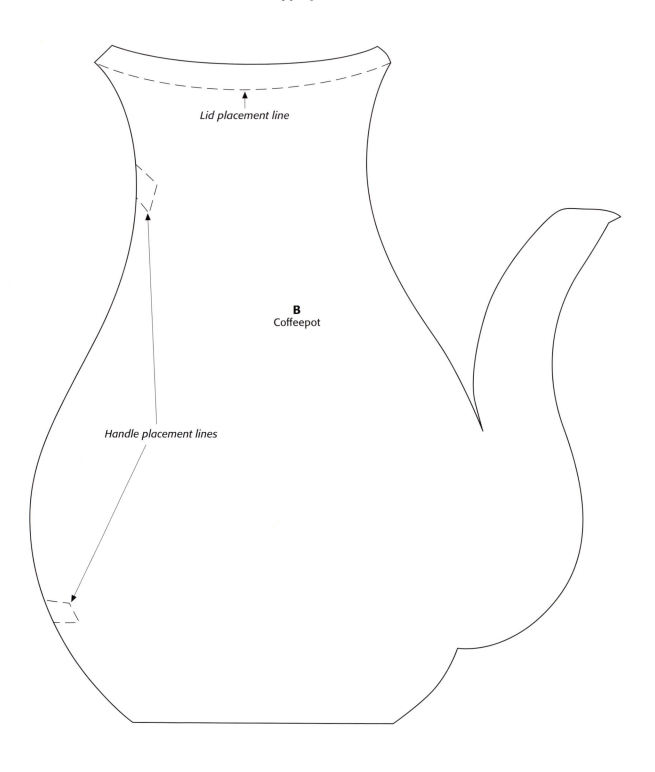

Lid placement line

B
Coffeepot

Handle placement lines

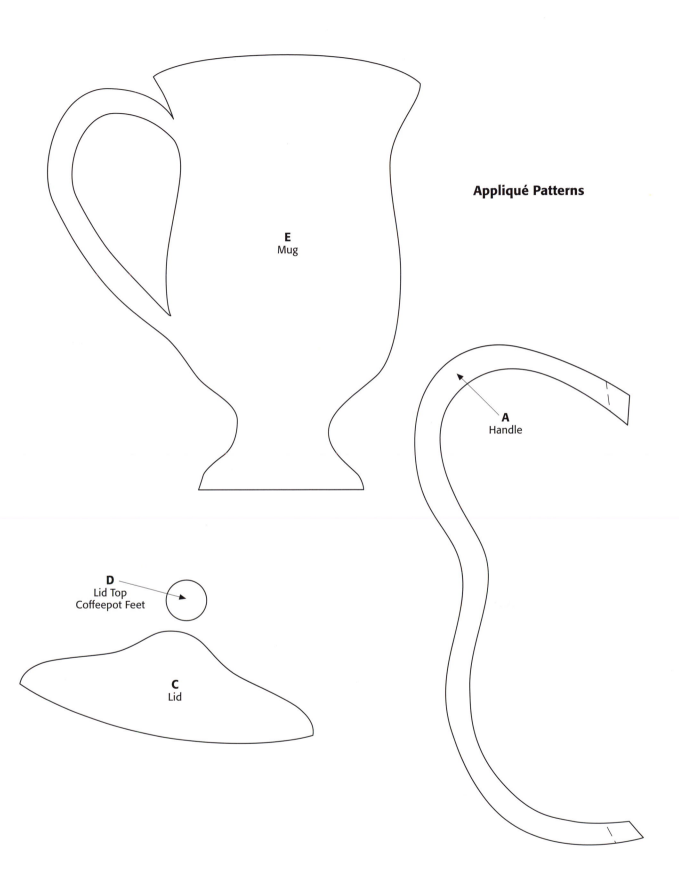

Appliqué Patterns

E
Mug

A
Handle

D
Lid Top
Coffeepot Feet

C
Lid

BLUEBERRY COFFEE CAKE

What could be easier than embellishing a cake mix with a few simple ingredients? No need for this one to cool down much. It's delicious when fresh and warm.

1½ cups fresh or frozen blueberries
⅓ cup water
½ cup granulated sugar
3 tablespoons cornstarch
1 package white cake mix
¼ cup (½ stick) plus 2 tablespoons butter
1 egg, beaten
¾ cup milk
1 teaspoon vanilla

1. Prepare the filling: In a medium saucepan mix blueberries and water and simmer covered about 5 minutes until the berries are tender. Combine the sugar and cornstarch and stir into the fruit. Cook and stir over medium heat until the mixture is thick and bubbly. Set filling aside.

2. Reserve ½ cup of the dry cake mix and set aside. Pour the remaining mix into a medium bowl and cut in ¼ cup butter until the mixture resembles coarse crumbs.

3. In another bowl combine the egg, milk, and vanilla. Add the egg mixture to the dry mixture and stir with a wooden spoon just until moistened. The batter will be lumpy.

4. Spread half of the batter into a greased 8" x 8" x 2" baking pan. Spread the filling over batter. Drop the remaining batter in small mounds onto the filling.

5. In another small bowl, cut 2 tablespoons butter into ½ cup of the reserved cake mix until crumbly. Sprinkle over the coffee cake.

6. Bake at 350° for about 40 to 45 minutes or until golden brown.

ABOUT THE AUTHOR

CATHY WIERZBICKI was introduced to the sewing machine early in life by her mother, who taught her how to sew simple garments that were entered into county fairs. What started as a lukewarm interest in quiltmaking in 1993 quickly evolved into a full-time passion.

Even though quilting has a prominent role in her life, Cathy has wide-ranging interests in crafts, sewing, needlework, decorative painting, and baking. In fact, to some who know her, Cathy is best known for baking delicious pies, so it is no stretch for her when she combines her love of quilting with her fondness for coffee time by serving up the recipes and quilts in this book.

With roots in Michigan, Cathy and her five siblings are scattered across the country. She has now relocated to Minnesota from the Pacific Northwest with Tom, her husband of 30 years. She has also lived in Texas and Iowa. She has two children, Tom and Stacey. In addition to publishing her own line of patterns, Cathy has two other books to her credit. This is her first book with Martingale & Company.

new and bestselling titles from

America's Best-Loved Craft & Hobby Books®

America's Best-Loved Quilt Books®

NEW RELEASES
20 Decorated Baskets
Asian Elegance
Batiks and Beyond
Classic Knitted Vests
Clever Quilts Encore
Crocheted Socks!
Four Seasons of Quilts
Happy Endings
Judy Murrah's Jacket Jackpot
Knits for Children and Their Teddies
Loving Stitches
Meadowbrook Quilts
Once More around the Block
Pairing Up
Patchwork Memories
Pretty and Posh
Professional Machine Quilting
Purely Primitive
Shadow Appliqué
Snowflake Follies
Style at Large
Trashformations
World of Quilts, A

APPLIQUÉ
Appliquilt in the Cabin
Artful Album Quilts
Blossoms in Winter
Color-Blend Appliqué
Garden Party
Sunbonnet Sue All through the Year

HOLIDAY QUILTS & CRAFTS
Christmas Cats and Dogs
Christmas Delights
Creepy Crafty Halloween
Handcrafted Christmas, A
Hocus Pocus!
Make Room for Christmas Quilts
Snowman's Family Album Quilt, A
Welcome to the North Pole

LEARNING TO QUILT
101 Fabulous Rotary-Cut Quilts
Casual Quilter, The
Fat Quarter Quilts
More Fat Quarter Quilts
Quick Watercolor Quilts
Quilts from Aunt Amy
Simple Joys of Quilting, The
Your First Quilt Book (or it should be!)

PAPER PIECING
40 Bright and Bold Paper-Pieced Blocks
50 Fabulous Paper-Pieced Stars
Down in the Valley
Easy Machine Paper Piecing
For the Birds
It's Raining Cats and Dogs
Papers for Foundation Piecing
Quilter's Ark, A
Show Me How to Paper Piece
Traditional Quilts to Paper Piece

QUILTS FOR BABIES & CHILDREN
Easy Paper-Pieced Baby Quilts
Even More Quilts for Baby
More Quilts for Baby
Play Quilts
Quilts for Baby
Sweet and Simple Baby Quilts

ROTARY CUTTING/SPEED PIECING
101 Fabulous Rotary-Cut Quilts
365 Quilt Blocks a Year Perpetual Calendar
1000 Great Quilt Blocks
Around the Block Again
Around the Block with Judy Hopkins
Cutting Corners
Log Cabin Fever
Pairing Up
Strips and Strings
Triangle-Free Quilts
Triangle Tricks

SCRAP QUILTS
Nickel Quilts
Rich Traditions
Scrap Frenzy
Spectacular Scraps
Successful Scrap Quilts

TOPICS IN QUILTMAKING
Americana Quilts
Bed and Breakfast Quilts
Bright Quilts from Down Under
Creative Machine Stitching
Everyday Embellishments
Fabulous Quilts from Favorite Patterns
Folk Art Friends
Handprint Quilts
Just Can't Cut It!
Quilter's Home: Winter, The
Split-Diamond Dazzlers
Time to Quilt

CRAFTS
300 Papermaking Recipes
ABCs of Making Teddy Bears, The
Blissful Bath, The
Creating with Paint
Handcrafted Frames
Handcrafted Garden Accents
Painted Whimsies
Pretty and Posh
Sassy Cats
Stamp in Color

KNITTING & CROCHET
365 Knitting Stitches a Year
  Perpetual Calendar
Basically Brilliant Knits
Crochet for Tots
Crocheted Aran Sweaters
Knitted Sweaters for Every Season
Knitted Throws and More
Knitter's Template, A
Knitting with Novelty Yarns
More Paintbox Knits
Simply Beautiful Sweaters for Men
Today's Crochet
Too Cute! Cotton Knits for Toddlers
Treasury of Rowan Knits, A
Ultimate Knitter's Guide, The

Our books are available at bookstores and your favorite craft, fabric, and yarn retailers. If you don't see the title you're looking for, visit us at **www.martingale-pub.com** or contact us at:

1-800-426-3126

International: 1-425-483-3313 • Fax: 1-425-486-7596 • Email: info@martingale-pub.com

For more information and a full list of our titles, visit our Web site.